Catalina Island Pottery and Tile
1927-1937
Island Treasures

Carole Coates
With Photography by Jeffrey B. Snyder

Schiffer Publishing Ltd

4880 Lower Valley Road, Atglen, PA 19310 USA

Designed by Bonnie M. Hensley
Cover design by Bruce M. Waters
Type set in HoratioDBol/Lydian BT

ISBN: 0-7643-1401-7
Printed in China
1 2 3 4

Published by Schiffer Publishing Ltd.
4880 Lower Valley Road
Atglen, PA 19310
Phone: (610) 593-1777; Fax: (610) 593-2002
E-mail: Schifferbk@aol.com
Please visit our web site catalog at
www.schifferbooks.com

This book may be purchased from the publisher.
Include $3.95 for shipping. Please try your bookstore first.
We are always looking for people to write books on new and related subjects. If you have an idea for a book please contact us at the above address.
You may write for a free catalog.

In Europe, Schiffer books are distributed by
Bushwood Books
6 Marksbury Avenue
Kew Gardens
Surrey TW9 4JF England
Phone: 44 (0) 20-8392-8585; Fax: 44 (0) 20-8392-9876
E-mail: Bushwd@aol.com
Free postage in the UK. Europe: air mail at cost.

Dedication

This book is dedicated to the memory of Jon Rippey, a visionary Catalina collector and friend, and to the many pottery and tile aficionados, Catalina-lovers, and fellow "research hounds" who have discovered a further meaning for Wrigley's slogan: "In all the world no trip like this."

Biography

Carole Coates, tile and pottery collector, historian, writer, lecturer, and native Californian is one of the leading experts and top collectors of Catalina Island pottery and tile. Inspired by idyllic childhood summers spent on Catalina Island, where like a baby duck she imprinted on the colorful wares surrounding her, she shares her expertise and insider tips garnered from 20 years of collecting and research. Contributor to Schiffer's *Bauer Pottery* and *Monterey Furniture* books, since 1995 she has dealt in Vintage California furnishings, with an emphasis on Catalina and Bauer pottery, and Monterey furniture. A former television producer, screenwriter, network and studio executive, she lives in Northern California's Wine Country and continues to research Catalina Island wares. Anyone with new information to further this study may contact her via email at potteryhound@aol.com, web site at potteryhound.com, or mail at P.O. Box 75, Kenwood, CA 95452.

Carole Coates.

The author (left), and her Catalina Cousin Julie leaning on a vintage tile wall. Avalon, California.

Contents

Acknowledgments

Many thanks to all the contributors who shared so generously of their collections and their time including, Jerry Kunz, Alan and Laurie Carter, Steven Hoefs, Sandra Puttnam, Lillian Stone, John Phelps, Paul Lenaburg and Phil Rubin, Barbara and Bob Crow, Kenneth DeHahn, Larry Harris, Caroline Renton, Mark Wiskow and Susan Strommer, Will Richards, and Ron Pyke. Thanks to Kathy Davis, Cam Hanna, Brian Kaiser, and Naomi Murdoch for all their indispensable help as well as to pottery guru Jack Chipman, tile sage Norman Karlson, and California crazed Steve Soukup for their advocacy and studies. Much appreciation to The Santa Catalina Island Company and the Catalina Island Museum, especially to Stacey Ott and Jeannine Pederson. A big thank you to Lee Rosenthal and the late Al Fridley for their ground breaking work and the many passions they inspired, as well as to the pioneering research and help of Patricia Moore that extended even to this book. Hats off to Jeff Snyder both for his beautiful photography and for lugging all that heavy equipment up so many stairs. A very special thanks is due "tile hugger" Bill Noonan who willingly volunteered to assist with both additional photography and last minute editing and whose help allowed me to both feed my children and complete this book. Much gratitude for the crucial assistance of the Hall family, including Mr. Don Hall, Johnette Eilert, Joan Kaylor, Nancy Fisher, Virginia Biroch, Frances Moore, and Leroy Hall, as well as to Ken Ozenghar, Frank Machado, Al Oldham, Millie Poindexter, my Catalina cousin Julie Huizenga, Maxine Jones, Pastor Lopez Sr., Roger Upton Jr., the late Johnny Wendle, and others whose recollections and family documents helped bring both important facts and colorful information to life. A debt of gratitude is due to Mr. David Renton for both historical grounding and his most generous sharing of family documents and photos, which helped provide important new information on the pottery which otherwise would not have come to light. And lastly thanks to my parents for giving me such special memories of Catalina summers, and to my wonderful children, Molly and Jackson, and their *patient* father, Mike Rosenfeld Sr., who have endured both my obsessions as a collector and my writing assignments with equal aplomb and even occasional interest.

Foreword

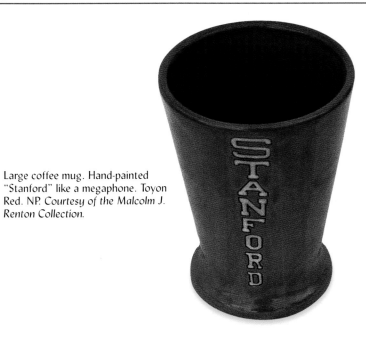

Large coffee mug. Hand-painted "Stanford" like a megaphone. Toyon Red. NP. *Courtesy of the Malcolm J. Renton Collection.*

Cowboy hat. Hand painted "Merry Xmas from D.M. Renton," dated "1934." Given as special gifts. Toyon Red. NP. *Courtesy of the Malcolm J. Renton Collection.*

by Mr. David Renton

Raised on Catalina Island where he loved to hike, fish, and water ski, Mr. Renton graduated from Avalon High School in 1964, then went on to Stanford and M.I.T. where he earned a Master in Business Administration. For many years he was Director and Vice President of the hotel division for one of the largest real estate organizations in the U.S., and since 1981 he has headed his own real estate investment and investment banking services firm.

A number of years ago my father, Malcolm Renton, gave me his prized Stanford University mug made of Catalina Island Pottery. Dad graduated from Stanford in 1929 and prior to that Avalon High School in 1925. This unique piece and a few others have special meaning to me not only because they were my father's, but because my grandfather, David M. Renton, was the driving force behind the development of Catalina tile and pottery products.

The original Tile Factory, and the Catalina Tile and Pottery Company that evolved from it, were departments of the Santa Catalina Island Company of which David Renton (best known as "D.M.") was Vice President and General Manager. As a master builder, he was very familiar with all types of building materials, and with this knowledge he identified the first clay deposits on the island. Encouraged by Mr. William Wrigley Jr., D.M. established the tile and pottery department within the company, directed its overall operations, hired the key employees and oversaw the sales and distribution network for the products. This is all documented in his correspondence with Mr. Wrigley.

The production and sale of quality tile and pottery at Catalina took the combined efforts of many highly talented people including the artists, craftsmen, chemists, laborers, salesmen, managers, and others. However, Carole Coates has asked me to give a personal perspective of my grandfather's involvement, and I think the best way to do this is to present a few key passages from his correspondence with William Wrigley Jr. and Philip K. Wrigley.

D.M. was often referred to as "the hands of William Wrigley" with the responsibility and authority to implement Mr. Wrigley's plans for the Island. William Wrigley Jr. was an extraordinary man, one of the preeminent businessmen of his day. Both he and my grandfather prided themselves on doing things others said could not be done, expected exceptional effort from themselves and the people that worked for them, and had outgoing personalities brimming with enthusiasm and humor. D.M. greatly admired William Wrigley Jr. and was proud to head up his Catalina interests. As they worked together a close personal friendship developed.

The clay products operation was of particular interest to both men. On June 6, 1927, D.M. wrote to William Wrigley, "Our Tile Plant will allow us to do some wonderful artistic work in our building program in the future, and within the next five years Catalina no doubt will undergo a wonderful change." This statement reflects the theme that D.M. had in mind for the development of the character of the resort community of Avalon. Mr. Wrigley confirmed this idea when on June 29, 1927 he wrote, "Your ideas and mine agree entirely... there is no doubt in the world about tile making Avalon a very attractive place, especially the tile roofs on the hillside homes." The idea was to introduce Spanish style architecture in a significant way using Catalina roof tile, floor tile, hollow tile, and decorative tile in construction and design. Having a large supply of materials readily available at low cost was a great advantage. It also introduced an important new industry to Catalina, one not dependent on tourism.

During the 1927-1928 period when the Tile Factory began operations, D.M. built, or was building, many homes and other structures on the island using Catalina tile. Some of the projects include: the Casino, the Catalina Country Club, the Toyon School for Boys, the homes on Tremont Street, the Bird Park structures, and the two homes he built for himself (Casa Del Monte which became the Philip Wrigley home, and then Casa Solana located adjacent to it).

In a letter to Mr. Wrigley on May 23, 1927, he wrote, "We are burning tile in our temporary kiln, but can only take care of 500 pieces at a time. It seems to be coming out very much better than we anticipated. By using some of the Fuller's Earth from the Isthmus with clays varying in type from our various sections, we find there is no shrinkage. That is something new in tile manufacture . . . The souvenirs we made up are going to work out in fine shape, I am confident. As you know, I have always been a strong proponent for the invention and sale of novelties pertaining directly to Catalina Island. I now think we have it, and it should prove later to be one of our best departments." The "souvenirs" and "novelties" created were the birth of Catalina pottery.

William Wrigley always gave D.M. his full backing and support. On January 12, 1932, Mr. Wrigley wrote to D.M., "I also believe that the clays on the Island will develop in a satisfactory manner into a manufacturing enterprise of note. The tile business has taken a tremendous stride forward.., but with you at the wheel, I do not think it is yet started." Sadly, in February of 1932, William Wrigley Jr. passed away. And a dramatic era in the history of Catalina came to a close. Philip K. Wrigley assumed control of the family interests at a difficult time. The Great Depression was impacting the nation.

Wanting to carry on the work of William Wrigley, D.M. personally acquired the Band Box Theater in 1933, which he completely reconstructed in the manner of Olvera Street in Los Angeles, using large amounts of Catalina tile and pottery. He wrote to Philip Wrigley on August 11, 1933, "Paseo de El Encanto seems to have made a big hit with everyone who comes to Avalon. I feel very proud of it...With the Spanish music we have there, it makes a real Catalina atmosphere, for as you know at one time this Island was a Spanish grant."

Between 1934 and 1938, Philip Wrigley expanded this effort by implementing a dramatic redesign of Crescent Avenue using what he termed an "Early California" theme, first with D.M.'s active involvement (until he retired in 1936) and then with my father's. Buildings along the waterfront were faced with Catalina tile; and a serpentine wall, large planters, and decorative tiled fountains were added. In addition, palm and olive trees were planted, and theme signage and other artistic additions were put in place. The new Pottery Shop was built on the waterfront across from the El Encanto providing an additional outlet for the sale of pottery and tile to island visitors.

My grandfather would be very pleased to know of the interest shown today in Catalina tile and pottery, products in which he took a great deal of personal pride. I congratulate Carole Coates for writing this fine book containing both new research and abundant photographs documenting the Catalina clay products industry. It is a work that I'm sure will be of great interest to Islanders, Island visitors, and tile and pottery collectors alike.

Casa Del Monte, the Phillip Wrigley home.

Casa Solana, the Renton home in the foreground. Casa del Monte and garage above right and left. *Courtesy of the Malcolm J. Renton Collection.*

Mr. William Wrigley Jr. and Mr. D.M. Renton relaxing at the Country Club. *Courtesy of the Malcolm J. Renton Collection.*

Introduction

Round Dragon tile designed for iron smoking stand. Glazed sides indicate a tile that can "stand alone." Red and yellow on black field. Very hard to find. 9" diameter. $950+. *Courtesy of Carole Coates.*

Red clay blocks with glazed letters spelling out "AVALON". 1" square. $50 each. *Courtesy of Alan & Laurie Carter.*

An Overview

The beautiful city of Avalon on Southern California's Catalina Island is perched on gentle hills inside a protected cove. A picturesque red tile roofed Moorish Casino impressively dominates one side of the bay and it appears that somehow on your 45 minute catamaran ride from San Pedro you might have been accidentally transported to an idyllic Mediterranean village. Robert Towne overcame writer's block on his movie script for "Chinatown" on Catalina's Isthmus, where simply the smell of the air channeled a long lost Los Angeles. Like many artists, writers, and visitors before and since, Catalina's nostalgic beauty supplied ample inspiration.

Over a million people every year do "travel on to Avalon," as one of over 60 songs written about the Island goes, but many day-trippers don't see beyond the souvenir shops to the real treasures, the richness and charm of a near lost California heritage that's embedded in stucco and lining the walls.

The story of Catalina pottery and tile begins with a little "Tile Factory" on Pebbly Beach, which started by producing industrial building products and evolved into making hand glazed art tile of extraordinary beauty. A Pottery Plant was created in 1930 as a separate entity called The Catalina Clay Products Company. It operated at the same location as the tile factory, and created pottery of amazing complexity, diversity, artistry and usefulness. Envisioned, championed, and overseen by D.M. Renton, backed by Mr. Wrigley, they called upon the expertise of top ceramists, used mainly indigenous materials and founded a cadre of local workers.

The Spanish Revival culminated in a tremendous renaissance of art and architecture and helped set the stage for Catalina's success. Not even the Great Depression could stop the enthusiasm of this burgeoning romantic era. Perhaps the colorful pottery, beautiful paintings, interesting textiles, and dramatic new building styles were

Avalon Bay.

America's optimistic antidote to the nation's bleak economic prospects, as banks started to close and jobs became scarce.

The decade long story of Catalina Island pottery and tile is almost as dramatic as a movie script. Set on an isolated romantic Isle, with a cast of interesting characters, taking place in a period of historic tumult and stress, with divergent styles from Moorish to Deco to Native American to Mexican and with all of this creative work overlapping at a frenzied pace. It makes for a much more fascinating and complex tale than our average depression era pottery chronology of ". . . and then we made."

Catalina's ceramic treasures are more fully appreciated within the context of the time, place, and cultural circumstances under which they were made, all of which helped contribute to its uniqueness as an art form. Although it seems remarkable to us today that this prolific array of Catalina's wares were created and produced in ten short years, even more amazingly the bulk of active decorative tile production at the Tile Factory occurred for only a five year span, from 1928 to 1932, while the main years for the Pottery Plant's production were the six years from 1930 to 1936. The fact that continual changes took place to satisfy the needs of the market, an enormous diversity of items were produced in both the tile and pottery lines, and the peak production years overlapped make a simple time-line documentation impossible and potentially inaccurate. We can certainly hope that with more recognition will come even more detailed information on the "who, when, what, and where" of specific contributions from ceramists, artists, and designers, but fortunately for us people wrote actual letters during the 1930s and the recently uncovered Wrigley-Renton correspondence has provided us with many of the up until now unknown inner workings of the tile factory and pottery plant by the sea.

The Deagan Chimes. Given to the city by Ada Wrigley in 1925. "Tiled up" in 1934 by Malcolm Renton. Later restored by RTK Studios.

Pacific Bell building in Avalon.

The Tile Factory's small beginning. 1927. *Courtesy of the Malcolm J. Renton Collection.*

An Island garden's "shrine" of pictorial and field tiles. *Courtesy of Sandra Puttnam.*

Frog bookends. 4" long by 4" high.
Green glaze. $2,000+. *Courtesy of
Carole Coates.*

"Fishnet" lamp. The lamp was named this in a
1932 press release, but known as a "rope"
lamp. Seafoam glaze with new custom shade.
$2,800+. *Courtesy of Carole Coates.*

Catalina oil jar, Toyon Red. 17" tall.
$1,100. *Courtesy of Carole Coates.*

Close up of ashtray holder set showing Toucan detail. Each of four sides was decorated with a different bird. Other sets did the same treatment with fish, or with deco flowers and each had a matching decorated cigarette box.

Handled candlestick. 4" across. Hand applied handle. Blue glaze. $150. *Courtesy of Carole Coates.*

Close up of "Kissing Birds" glazed plate showing detail and glaze separation. *Courtesy of Jerry Kunz.*

A "Pottery Shop" sold Catalina wares on Casino Way in Avalon from the early 1930s. Pottery and tile was also sold on the Island at the Bird Park, the Island Villas, the Arcade, and in a shop at the Casino. *Courtesy of the Malcolm J. Renton Collection.*

A Colorful History

From Canoes to Steamships

Santa Catalina Island lies 22 miles off Southern California's coast, not the 26 miles made famous by song. The Island is 21 miles long and no more than 8 miles wide at any point. It is one of the eight Channel Islands, sometimes called "America's Galapagos." Catalina is home to indigenous animals and plants, as well as teeming ocean and bird life. Long known as a favorite mooring spot for boaters, and a top destination for scuba divers and sports fishermen, it's also a family vacation get away as wholesome as a time trip to the 1950s. The latest resurgence of interest in Catalina surrounds its legacy as home to one of California's twentieth century ceramic treasures, the vintage tile and art pottery made on the Island.

The romantic and dramatic credentials of Catalina Island are plentiful. From it's first Native American inhabitants, the Pemú'nga, whose rich seagoing culture was tragically ended by the Spanish Mission system, to the arrival of the European "discoverers" Cabrillo in 1592 and Viscaino in 1602. After becoming one of the last Spanish land grants in 1846, an assortment of shepherds, smugglers, sea pirates, and gold seekers sought their fortune or eked out a living.

A series of owners followed during the late 1800s, until General Phineas Banning, a developer of ports, shipping, and stagecoach lines, and his sons gave the Island its first incarnation as a tourist resort. The crystal blue waters, teaming ocean life, and temperate climate, to this day not as hot or cold (or smoggy!) as Los Angeles, were popular attractions. Hotels and road development followed but a disastrous fire in 1915 ended their adventure.

Mr. William Wrigley Jr. bought the Island in 1919.

Lively colors and vintage furnishings in a contemporary home. *Courtesy of Allan and Laurie Carter.*

Spanish style home overlooking Avalon Bay.

Mr. William Wrigley Jr. (b.1861, d.1932)
A Happy Man

William Wrigley Jr., one of the most successful businessmen of his day, was just not cut out for school. Born in Philadelphia in 1861, perhaps his uncommon energy and enthusiasm is what caused him to be branded a troublemaker. His formal education came to a screeching halt in eighth grade and his father soon put him on the road with a horse and buggy selling Wrigley's Scouring Soap. As a salesman, he was a natural. Maybe you suspect that your own "challenging" child is simply filled with the gumption that helped propel the entrepreneurial Mr. Wrigley to the top? If you are that hopefully optimistic, then there's someone out there who's got a "Catalina" tile table they'd like to sell you.

William Wrigley Jr. married Ada Foote and they moved to Chicago in 1891 where he started his own soap business. He added baking powder to his line and as a premium offered two sticks of free gum with every package. You know the rest of the story. Wrigley's Spearmint and Juicy Fruit gums were America's favorites by 1910. Wrigley was the father of product "branding," used incentive premiums to great effect, and was one of the first believers in the fledgling concept of advertising. Shrewd investments and diversification caused his fortune to grow but all that knew him speak of him with great respect, reverence, and genuine warmth. The philanthropic example set by Mr. and Mrs. William Wrigley Jr., was carried on by their sons and daughters, and continues to this day through the works of his grandchildren and great-grandchildren.

William Wrigley Jr. was in his fifties and at the stage in life when he was comfortable enough in his success to enjoy it a bit. "I'm a happy man myself," he said. "I want to make others happy." (Bushing 1994) It was in this state of mind that Mr. Wrigley came to Catalina Island.

Portrait of William Wrigley Jr. *Courtesy of the Santa Catalina Island Company.*

Lady Spanish Dancer hand painted plate. Signed with initials attributed to Graham. 10". $750+. *Courtesy of Allan & Laurie Carter.*

Olvera Street Pottery Shop, in Los Angeles, circa 1931. All Catalina was displayed on Monterey Furniture, another colorful southern California creation. Both Monterey and Catalina were sold together at Barker Brothers Department Store in Los Angeles and other cities. *Courtesy of the Malcolm J. Renton Collection.*

"Arches of Mission. San Juan Capistrano." Hand painted plate. 10". Signed "G" for Graham. $550. *Courtesy of Carole Coates.*

The Spanish Revival Movement
A Colorful Revolution

Meanwhile on the mainland, or "overtown" as Islanders say, there was a revolution going on. The public became fascinated with all things "Old California." This "Spanish Revival" all stemmed from a highly romanticized view of the days when California was in Spain and then Mexico's hands. Popular books such as *Ramona*, and movies like *Old Arizona* fueled fantasies about when the "Californios" ruled the land. It was a time that never existed except in people's imaginations, days filled with fiestas, as señors and señoritas, vaqueros and caballeros, strummed their guitars, danced, or worked on their ranchos.

It is believed that the Spanish Revival Movement actually began in 1915 with the Panama-California International Exposition in San Diego. The buildings were designed in a "Southern California Hispanic Style" and used a profusion of colorful Moorish influenced decorative tiles inside and out. The tiles were designed and created by a renowned English expert named Fred Wilde, a name that will resurface again on Catalina Island.

The crumbling California Missions were rebuilt and the Avila Adobe, the oldest existing residence in Los Angeles, was brought back from ruin in 1926 to become "Olvera Street," soon to be home to a shop that sells "Catalinaware."

There was a building boom underway in the Golden State and all these Spanish style homes needed something to put in them. Monterey furniture was created by a Los Angeles firm and was a top seller, with some pieces incorporating Catalina tiles. Red tile pavers were used on interior and exterior floors, as well as the requisite red roofing tiles. Decorative tiles in bright "Mexican fiesta" colors were used extensively as accents, whether in the forms of murals installed in entries, random patterns placed on patio walls, stair runners, mantles, alcoves, fountains, entries, or the obvious kitchens and bathrooms.

Tiles installed in stucco at the Island's Airport in the Sky.

Paver tiles with glazed inserts on walkway.

Star tile stair risers. *Courtesy of Dr. Staff.*

Single Green Parrot mural.

Kitchen alcove done in yellow and black tile. Original installation. *Courtesy of Sandra Puttnam*

The Hands of Mr. Wrigley
Mr. David M. Renton (b. 2/8/1887, d. 5/27/1947)

When William Wrigley Jr. bought Catalina sight unseen he had no idea he would spend the last twelve years of his life, and so much money, improving it, but he did know the man to help him do the job: David M. Renton, known by all simply as D.M. Mr. Wrigley called him one morning with his usual enthusiasm and friendliness, "I have just bought Catalina Island. How would you like to go over and do the building?" It would become D.M.'s life's work. (Wendell 1939, 111-113)

The combination of Wrigley and Renton lit a spark in Avalon. In a frenzy of activity, homes, hotels, exotic amusements, travel, and the necessary infrastructure were built. Mr. Wrigley dreamed up the "Package Deal" and provided everything from boat to bed for one fair price. The younger generation of Phillip Wrigley and Malcolm Renton would continue in the same spirit during the 1930s and '40s, "branding" the

Mr. D.M. Renton, the "father" of Catalina Island pottery and tile in the 1920s, sitting at Mount Ada and making notes of future projects. *Courtesy of the Malcolm J. Renton Collection.*

town much like Wrigley's Chewing Gum, using the skills of graphic artist Otis Shepard and blasting an "Airport in the Sky" into existence on the top of a mountain, with seaplanes taking off and landing at an amphibious airport. Didn't these people ever take siestas?

In 1926 William's son Phillip (P.K.) Wrigley was made President of the Wrigley Chewing Gum Company and William Wrigley Jr. focused his instinctual promotional abilities to fire up the public's imagination about the Island. He made it seem closer, friendlier, and more accessible. He had already added the beautiful S.S. *Catalina* "Steamer" to their shipping line, held a Channel Swimming Contest with a $25,000 prize, as well as water-skiing contests, fishing tournaments, and golf championships. He brought his beloved Chicago Cub's baseball team to Avalon for Spring Training. Publicity releases helped to build Catalina's allure as the "Island of Romance" and soon it was a must-see attraction for visitors to Southern California as well as the world leaders, Presidents, and dignitaries. In this era before jet travel, Catalina was *the* Movie Star Colony, and provided a secluded retreat for all the top stars of the day, including Wrigley friend Charlie Chaplin. Author and sport fisherman Zane Grey built an Adobe style mansion on an Avalon hillside, as did movie cowboy Tom Mix.

D.M. Renton's expertise in building many exemplary Pasadena Craftsman style homes, as well as such diverse projects as Los Angeles' Mount Wilson Observatory in 1914, was all brought to bear on his Island projects. D.M. traveled the country to bring the best and brightest ideas back to Avalon, including a boardwalk modeled on Atlantic City, and an 18 hole golf course and Country Club based on a famous course at French Lick, Indiana. D.M. had a vision for the pottery and tile works. There is little doubt that he was its guiding force. Of the many remarkable things accomplished by Wrigley and Renton on Catalina, the ceramics created on Pebbly Beach, almost forgotten by the 1970s, will perhaps prove to be one of the most enduring and popular aspects of the Island's legacy.

Shepard designed luggage tag.

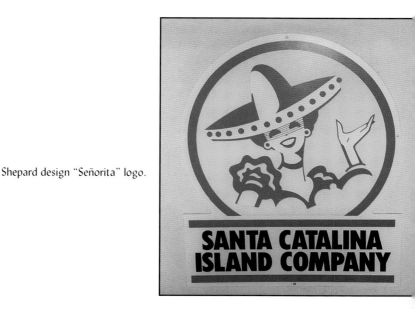

Shepard design "Señorita" logo.

Otis Shepard designed matchbook.

Catalina's amphibian airport at Hamilton Cove in the early 1930s. *Courtesy of the Malcolm J. Renton Collection.*

Airport in the Sky's control tower.

C-28—Steamers "Catalina" and "Avalon" at Pier, and Casino,

Avalon Bay, Santa Catalina, California

SA-H862

Vintage Postcard.

ENJOYING LIFE AT AVALON,
CATALINA ISLAND, CALIFORNIA   T10

Vintage Postcard.

A Factory by the Sea

Red Clay Beginnings: 1927-1928

The urban myth that Mr. Wrigley's car became mired in clay and was responsible for launching the pottery and tile works reads like one of the florid PR embellishments of the time. Cars and coaches became mired not once but many times over the years on the rugged adobe roads, but the story came to life for the public when Mr. Wrigley was driving the car.

Clay and mineral oxides were discovered during the many attempts to drill wells for fresh water, a major concern on a semi-arid Island. Using clay from many Island locations the "Tile Factory" officially began in April 1927 when machinery arrived to automate the brick and tile making process at nearby Pebbly Beach. Some bricks had been made by hand prior to this time, but what could be better than tile roofs for a town that had a prior and disastrous reputation for fires. (Wrigley-Renton correspondence)

A Mr. Stueve was brought from L.A. as superintendent and he hired five "experienced Mexican tile workers." Local legend has it that these men were from Aqua Caliente in Tijuana, a resort decorated extensively with colorful Mexican tiles. It's true that some of the earliest dark red clay decorative tiles look very much like Mexican tiles of the day.

The long-standing tradition of tile and pottery making in Mexico obviously had a direct impact on California. Tile "wizard" Rufus Keeler, of Malibu Pottery fame, cites the artistry of ". . . Mexico, where some of the most magnificent achievements in the use of tiles are to be seen to this day." (Ceramic Art of the Malibu Potteries, Keeler speech, 1926)

Pottery Plant and Tile Factory showing the entire complex as well as mining operations in the foreground.
Courtesy of the Catalina Island Museum.

Catalina brick, roofing and floor tile was used to build San Pedro City Hall, Clark Hall at Pomona College, and the Long Beach Auditorium. (Wrigley-Renton correspondence). The brick making became more sophisticated with different colors such as Avalon Tapestry, Catalina Bark, and Descanso Tapestry. These bricks can still be seen today topping many Avalon buildings and stucco walls.

"Buffalo" and Mexican style tiles done with very indistinct glaze separation. Two patterns. 5 7/8". Other 1930s companies made "Buffalo" knock off tiles. $250 each. *Courtesy of Carole Coates.*

Vintage Postcard. Aqua Caliente, Mexico spa and resort, c. 1930s.

Brick checkerboard effect with different colors topping stucco wall near Avalon High School.

Island Inspired Souvenirs
A Novel Idea

In 1927, under the umbrella of the tile factory, the first pottery items were made on the Island. They were novelties reflecting images of the Island's history and setting. First to be tried were "paperweights," tile shaped plaques of glass bottom boats or flying fish, and bookends featuring Catalina goats and cowboys. These were dark red clay molded pieces, not glazed but "tinted" in a copper green wash. A female artist was set up in the Hotel Atwater's Arcade to "paint" them there as an additional attraction for the tourists, a concept that would someday include artists painting decorative plates in public view. By November 1928, both bookends and Indian Head plaques were being sold on the Island and on the mainland. (Wrigley-Renton correspondence)

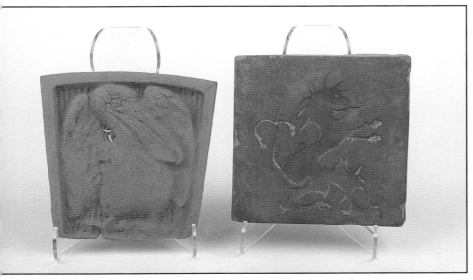

Very early Pelican and Lion tiles, red brick clay. Both 5 5/8" across. Lion is 1 1/8" thick. $200 & $150. Courtesy of Carole Coates.

William Wrigley bust tile. Very early "Made at Catalina" mark in script. Green copper patina. Red clay. 3 7/8" x 3 1/8". NP. Courtesy of The Catalina Island Museum.

Early Lotus decorative border tile, buff clay, non-original frame. $85. 2" x 5 7/8". $125. *Courtesy of Allan and Laurie Carter.*

Flying Fish plaque. "Flying Fi[sh] Catalina Island" on front. "Avalon. June 15. 1933. L.C.J." inscribed on back. 4 [?] across. Made from the earlie[st] days and usually found unglazed. Blue glaze. This o[ne] was said to be placed by the maid at each place setting a[s a] special occasion memento fo[r] dinner guests at Casa Del Monte, P.K. Wrigley's residence. NP. *Courtesy of Steven Hoefs.*

Frolicking Goats bookend, copper patina over green glaze, very early red brick clay. Signed "Catalina." 6 1/4" high. NP. *Courtesy of Steven Hoefs.*

Early "See No Evil" Three Monkey's bookend. Red brick clay, recent black paint. 4" x 5"wide. Buyer beware, these have been reproduced very recently. $225 single. *Courtesy of Allan and Laurie Carter.*

Earliest Influences: The Malibu Connection

Trying to unearth the true story of Catalina Island pottery and tile is like going on an archeological dig. Shards of information surface, you brush them off and try to fit them into the puzzle but there are still many missing and confusing pieces. Unlike some firms that had only one or two ceramists who also functioned as plant supervisors for the life of the company, Catalina employed many ceramists, supervisors, and consultants in overlapping time frames and in different areas of production. During the peak years for the tile factory and pottery plant they had separate "supervisors," at other slower times one person supervised both operations.

Many prominent ceramists and workmen in this industry leapfrogged from company to company and some were "loaned" for periods of time to relieve financial stress. As industry colleagues many of these men were acquainted and shared information regarding jobs, trends, and technical information. It was similar to "networking" today. It paid to help others, they might be in a position to hire or recommend you.

The influences the major California pottery and tile works had on each other, Catalina, Bauer, Pacific, Metlox, Gladding McBean, and the Malibu Tile Works are obvious to an educated eye, and certainly there are many subtle relationships as well between some of the smaller companies such as Caliente, Padre, Tudor, Poxon, and Cemar. But what might not be as obvious is the strong, until this date unproven, connection between Catalina and Malibu potteries.

Both Catalina and Malibu made almost identical items using similar techniques in their early years and now it is clear why. Rufus Keeler historian Brian Kaiser has extensively interviewed Mr. Keeler's niece and other relatives, and their consistent recollections are Mr. Keeler (d. 1934), one of the top ceramists of his day, "took the ferry" over to Catalina to "help them out" on a regular basis, not as an employee but as a "consultant" during Catalina's early years. This information dovetails perfectly with Malibu's operating years of 1926 to 1932 and the fact that Mr. Keeler traveled "home" from Malibu to Southgate on weekends leaving him plenty of time to moonlight at Catalina. It is also possible that this "consulting" coincided with layoffs at Malibu the first of which occurred in July or August of 1929. According to employee J. Donald Prouty it was a "'shutdown' . . . [but was] termed a "temporary layoff." This might have been another factor that brought or introduced additional Malibu employees to Catalina as well. (Malibu Potteries 1988, 45)

It's unlikely that D.M. Renton *wouldn't* have made the pilgrimage to Malibu Pottery and met Mr. Keeler on one of his many information gathering trips, perhaps even on his way to tour the Santa Barbara Biltmore in 1929 to view the stunning Spanish style architecture and the impressive Gladding McBean tile murals that still grace it's walls. D.M. was diligent in his research with top experts in the state, even consulting with ceramic engineers at Stanford when he went to visit his son Malcolm at college. (Wrigley-Renton correspondence)

Another important connection to Malibu comes with Charles (C.E.) Mason, the superintendent of Malibu Pottery, who was also employed by Catalina for a short time, perhaps along with Mr. Keeler on a consulting basis. Mr. Mason had been a mold maker at Gladding McBean where Mr. Keeler was also employed. Mr. Mason trained his stepson, Don Ruth, in the art of mold making and Mr. Ruth was employed by Catalina for all of its production years, and is responsible for many of its famous molded creations.

Other evidence that links the two potteries comes in ceramic form. Some items made by both firms are identical and others very similar. Malibu made an Indian Head tile plaque that is a twin to Catalina's late 1928 version (other than the different company names featured on the top front), as well as highly similar "cuenca" paver tiles, and a Malibu Lion's Head fountain piece that is of similar design to Catalina's Lion head tile/bookends. Pottery items that mirror Malibu include Moorish raised design plates and Monk Bookends (Catalina's version are slightly smaller than Malibu's) as well as lamps. The Monk Bookends done by both Malibu and Catalina were preceded by Gladding McBean's even larger version made of Lincoln, California, clay. Mr. Keeler and Mr. Mason worked for Gladding McBean in Lincoln in 1909. Other Keeler connections come with "Eve" bookends produced earlier when Keeler was at the "CALCO" Tile Company. Many Catalina tiles produced in the early 1930s reflect both the Malibu esthetic and a similar production technique, albeit with different glazes. The single Marlin tile in particular is of quite a remarkable quality, as are some early star tiles. It is hoped that this book will lead to collaborating proof in pinpointing the exact time frame and attributions for Mr. Keeler and Mr. Mason's consulting work with Catalina. It seems ironic and wonderful that the two "potteries by the sea" can now be known for having more than the ocean in common.

Despite the existence of some "secret" recipes for glazes held under lock and key, it is important to note that many glazes were shared freely between colleagues. A difficult-to-develop "red" glaze with an underburn was born at Malibu and resembles Catalina's Toyon Red in an amazing way. Brian Kaiser tells us that Rufus Keeler often wrote "Fred Wilde gave me this . . ." and "Fred Wilde gave me that . . ." in reference

Indian Head tile plaque. 6 " x 4 " on red clay, hand painted at El Encanto, molded signature "Catalina Island" on front. Watch out for recent reproductions. NP. *Courtesy of Allan and Laurie Carter.*

to glazes he was using, and with that there is another connection back to Catalina via the Wilde family. Fred's son John was "loaned" to Catalina from 1931 to 1936 from Pomona Tile, and we find John referred to in 1931 as the "tile factory superintendent" (Wendle 1931, 123) and then in later years as the pottery plant supervisor. D.M. Renton built many homes in Pomona and also had a family connection to the Pomona Colleges. It has been suggested by David Renton that his Grandfather's building experience in this city would have put him in contact with Pomona Tile.

Mr. Stueve resigned in May 1928, but by June D.M. had found a "new man" to take over the tile factory. (Wrigley-Renton correspondence). Color saturated pottery and tile were on their way.

Moorish plate. Raised lines separate the blue, green, and yellow glaze colors. $500+. Courtesy of Jerry Kunz.

Top right: Monk bookends. Blue glaze, signed "Catalina." Very heavy. Similar to Malibu and Gladding McBean. $1,000+. Courtesy of Jerry Kunz.

Center right: "Eve" Deco bookends. Very early clay and "Catalina Isle" mark on front, low-fire gold finish. These are very similar to the bookends made by "Calco." NP. Courtesy of Paul Lenaburg &Phillip Rubin.

Bottom right: Rarely seen off the Island. Single Marlin tile, very detailed in execution, contemporary wooden frame. 12" x 6". NP. Courtesy of Steven Hoefs.

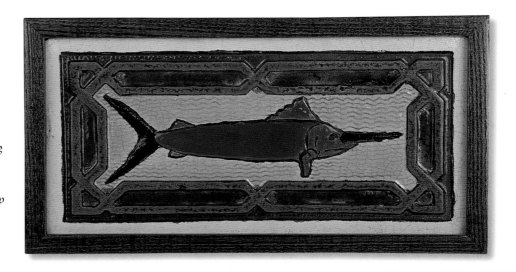

"Cuenca style" Lion tile. Cobalt glaze insert on red brick clay. 5 5/8". $250. *Courtesy of Allan and Laurie Carter.*

Color Arrives
Blended Glazes

The first glazed tiles came out of the factory in September of 1928. A Mr. Birchfield was employed from June 1928 until October 1929 directly from Pacific Clay Products company, a big L.A. firm, and was known for "working in glazes." (Whitaker Interview 2000) Mr. Renton went to tour the Pacific plant and see him in action prior to his joining Catalina. Harold Johnson also joined Catalina from Pacific in 1928 and it seems likely that Mr. Birchfield brought him along. It is not known if the wonderful early "blended" glazes found on Catalina's garden ware, often incorrectly identified as

Four assorted early tiles and backs. One Mexican style, the rest all done in a very high quality reminiscent of Malibu tiles. Dark red clay. *Courtesy of Carole Coates.*

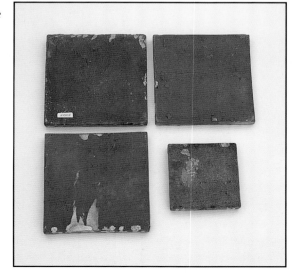

Three Pacific blended glaze pieces and bottom ink stamp. Similar in execution to Catalina's for a brief time. *Courtesy of Mark Wiskow and Susan Strommer.*

an "experimental glaze," was an invention of Mr. Johnson's, Mr. Birchfield's, or simply a use of techniques they had used at their last job. What is obvious is that the glazes on the first pieces of Catalina pottery to come out of the plant bore a close resemblance to early Pacific ware.

Two large oil jars from this period are sitting on Catalina Island at the Airport in the Sky. Island residents have said that these jars were a gift to Ada Wrigley from the pottery plant workers. Whether she or others had them put at the Airport, the gesture could either be seen as placing them in a position of prominence or as the equivalent of putting them behind the garage. This wild glazing technique might be an acquired taste, but modern-day admirers find many of the combinations quite striking. The forms done in this manner include a very limited number of vase shapes, spittoons, "Spanish" garden pots, and saucers. The pieces are much heavier than you'd expect for their size since they were made of a very dense brick-like clay. A circular early ink stamp, only one of three used on the Island, is found on these pieces. Glaze combinations are also found in limited numbers on later forms, but usually involve a combination of only two glaze colors.

Early "Catalina Island" ink stamp mark on blended glaze piece.

Three early blended glaze vases. Island mark in ink "Catalina Island." This is the most commonly found form for this glaze technique. $600+ depending on execution. *Courtesy of Sandra Puttnam.*

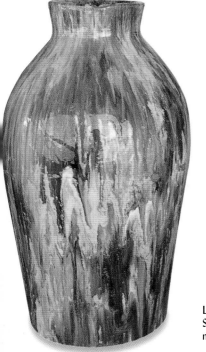

Blended glaze vases, two forms, Blue and yellow mottled effect. 9" and 7"tall. $500+. *Courtesy of Jerry Kunz.*

Large oil jar at Airport in The Sky. Blended glaze, one of a matching pair. NP.

Early flower pot. Blended glaze. 6" high. Yellow & turquoise glazes. $175. *Courtesy of Carole Coates.*

Blended glaze vase, green, yellow, and brown combination. $600. *Courtesy of Carole Coates.*

Crimped edge planter saucer. Blue, yellow, and green. 9" high. $100. *Courtesy of Jerry Kunz.*

Three unique early bulbous vases. Unique transitional or experimental technique with incised lines and different glazes. One two-toned with mottled cobalt. NP. *Courtesy of Steven Hoefs.*

Blended glaze tall mug and step vase. 6" high and 4" high. These slightly later forms might represent a transitional period. Normally only two colors were blended on these pieces. $225 & $500+. *Courtesy of Jerry Kunz.*

Unusual footed vase and common vase, done in rare mottled cobalt. Three early bulbous vases for comparison. Ranging from 7" to 5". NP. *Courtesy of Steven Hoefs.*

Roofing tile production doubled to 8,000 a day under Birchfield, which was very timely since the Casino roof would require over 80,000 alone. Patio and floor pavers were incised with designs and filled with colored glazes in the "cuenca" technique for use in the entry and balcony. A dramatic "bar" (actually a soda fountain since it was Prohibition) used all Catalina paver and single glaze tiles. By September of 1928, D.M. was looking forward to seeing his first kiln of "enamel" or glazed tile, done in octagonal shapes and single colors, intended for the Casino bathrooms. (Wrigley-Renton correspondence) One worker remembers the factory being on around the clock shifts in order to complete the Casino in time for the grand opening on May 1929. (Oldham 2000)

Tiled water fountain with many rarely seen paver tiles and borders. Sand Trap Restaurant, Avalon.

Hexagonal tiles in various colors. Some marked. $25 each. *Courtesy of Carole Coates.*

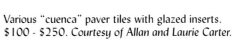

Various "cuenca" paver tiles with glazed inserts. $100 - $250. *Courtesy of Allan and Laurie Carter.*

Catalina's Casino.

The Moorish-Mediterranean style Casino, at twelve stories and 140 feet high, was the tallest building then existing in Los Angeles County. Never intended for gambling, it was home to the "Big Bands" in the 1930s and live radio broadcasts by 1934. The theater was the first in the world designed for "talkies." It won an award for architectural excellence for its unique cantilever design. Artist and scenic designer John Gabriel Beckman (who this author had the pleasure of knowing in the 1980s) was already well regarded for his work on classic movies such as *Casablanca* and the murals for Grauman's Chinese Theater. He designed and oversaw the gorgeous deco-style murals that still grace the inside of the theatre. The "underwater garden" tile murals he planned for the entry alcove were not completed in time (did someone say "over budget?") and were painted in. Contemporary tile designer Richard Keit finally completed the central "mermaid" mural panel with Mr. Beckman's supervision some fifty years later.

In October of 1929, Mr. Birchfield was let go because he "wasn't performing satisfactorily." Hopefully it wasn't the big oil jars at the airport that did him in. The U.S. Stock Market wasn't performing too well either. This was the month of the big "crash," and the tile plant was cut down to a very small crew. (Wrigley-Renton correspondence) Mr. Johnson left as well, and worked for Bauer pottery briefly in 1930. California pottery historian Jack Chipman surmises that the rings on Mr. Johnson's hand thrown flowerpots might have provided the inspiration for Bauer's famous "ring" dinnerware line. Whether Pacific, Catalina, or Bauer were first with colorful dinnerware has not been proven, but certainly this is a connection in the Pacific to Catalina to Bauer direction.

Clays of Many Colors: 1929

Like shards coming out of the sand at Pebbly Beach after a storm, new details on Catalina come up everyday. There is a lot of new information about what is "Island clay." Many people believe that only "red" clay was found on the Island, and that red and brown are the only "Island Clays." Letters from Mr. Renton to Mr. Wrigley indicate that in December of 1929 white clay *was* discovered on Catalina Island while drilling for water in a tunnel on the Summit. In D.M.'s opinion "the enamel takes very much better on the white than the red." (Wrigley-Renton correspondence)

The "urban myth" surrounding Mr. Wrigley's insistence on using "Island clay" is another area of debate. Many believe that only with Wrigley's death was mainland clay allowed. It is know that Mr. Wrigley "preferred" Island materials, but the importation of white clay from the mainland has been documented even in 1931, before the death of Mr. Wrigley. Writings from this time indicate that "practically all" of the clay was from the Island. You notice they didn't say *all*. (Wendle 1931, 123) Since a major part of the publicity focus was pottery made on the Island *of the Island*, i.e. "take home a little piece of the Island," it is understandable that the importation of clay would not have been publicized. White clay was brought from Lincoln, California, in quantity when dinnerware production became the factory's mainstay. Mr. Wrigley's passing probably made it easier to explain the "sudden" change.

Catalina tile backs showing three different clay colors. Dark red, medium red, and white.

Collecting Basics

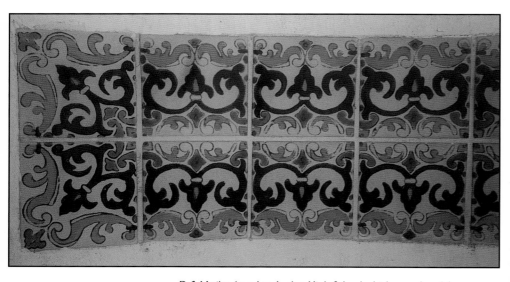

D & M tiles found at Avalon High School which was closed for earthquake repairs and remodeled in 1934 by a mainland contractor.

But is it Catalina?
Myths

If there's one myth that every Catalina tile and pottery lover would like to explode it's that every tile table, no matter what maker, is "Catalina." Catalina does have cachet and their tables bring higher prices than many other makers. One of the biggest rip-offs for innocent collectors is when even well meaning dealers sell tables as "Catalina," and up until now it was hard to prove them wrong. Some Catalina tile tables were made with iron and wooden bases manufactured on the Island, and these are easy to spot. The wooden tables usually have a special metal figure eight connector. The Island-iron tables known thus far are all identified in the captions of this book, but the distinctive "spoon" end on the gaming table bases do stand out as a unique feature. Even Lee Rosenthal's ground breaking book on Catalina tile contains several tables since discovered to be made by Taylor Tilery and others. Some Island installations contain D & M tile and are mistaken for Catalina. Bachelder Tile from Pasadena was used in the 1920s above the Post Office entrance of the Avalon Arcade and in private homes. Tile tables made in California have over thirty potential makers (Taylor, Tudor, D & M, and Hispano-Moresque are the more commonly confused ones) and sellers who sell a table as "Catalina?" or the often heard "The guy who sold it to me swore it was Catalina," or even "It's a Catalina 'style' tile table" should be sent to tile purgatory. There is no Catalina "Style" except the town of Avalon itself. There is no "generic Catalina" either, just like there is no generic Island out in the Pacific Ocean. Make sure to get genuinely expert advice before buying a "Catalina" tile table.

Another pet peeve for Catalina collectors is that all Island pottery is "rare." Many dinnerware items were produced in very large quantities and so were some vases in the "Floral Line." Some purists call this later phase "industrial artware," but a fairer term would be "industrious" artware. Unlike our current day image of a "factory," Catalina made items that ran the gamut of production techniques, from pure hand workmanship to factory-line output and everything in between. With the advent of the Internet, Catalina Island pottery is now available to collectors around the country in a way that has not been possible since the plants heyday. Through photos and descriptions, this book will help discern between items that are true rarities and those that are merely hard to find, and will inform readers about the most popular "common" items.

The last and most stubborn Catalina myth is that red clay is the only "Island clay," produced the best results, and commands the highest prices. Many brown, pink, white, and buff clays were indeed "Island clays." Advanced collectors rarely judge pieces based on their clay color, but on execution. Some white clay pieces are indeed superior to their red clay cousins, while other excellent pieces were only made in white clay.

Inside pottery plant's inventory room. *Courtesy of the Malcolm J. Renton Collection.*

Detail of Catalina-made wooden table base. Metal bracket in an "8" shape attaches the base to the legs. This is NOT a guarantee that the tiles in such a base are Catalina. They may have been replaced.

Assortment of molded figural ashtrays done on white clay. *Courtesy of Carole Coates.*

Pricing and Glazes

Catalina Island pottery and tile pricing is an occult art. Pricing depends on many factors including condition, form, and glaze color. The way pieces are marked makes no difference in pricing (see below). Catalina buyers tend to be more forgiving of condition in general since finding pristine examples is sometimes difficult because of the tendency of the soft brown and red clay bodies to chip. Lighter clay pieces are usually held to a higher standard and should be in mint condition. Pricing in this book reflects a good, not excellent condition, with very minor factory flaws, if any. Price adjustments are included for rarer glazes. Pieces with extreme glaze flaws, hairline cracks of any kind, and major chips will not bring even half retail. Restoration, even expertly done, affects pricing negatively and, if not disclosed, is automatic grounds for a return. Visible restorations are the kiss of death. Desirability can affect prices a great deal and sometimes have nothing to do with rarity. Some extremely rare items (such as "after hours" projects done by employees or extremely experimental pieces) are only of interest to scholarly collectors, while other more common vases or dinnerware forms are quite popular and desirable.

Auctions, both Internet and regular, are not reliable for gauging value. Depending on who's on vacation or whose stocks are down, a bidding war one week and tax time the next, prices will fluctuate wildly. Sometimes rare pieces go begging, and common pieces hit the roof. Misinformation is rampant. The most common practice is for buyers to state an early "made before" date that is either incorrect or that is applied to an example that was made throughout the life of the pottery in order to make it seem "rarer." Other sellers purposely do not state damage or repair in order to deceive. Your best assurance of a "good deal" is not to get the lowest price, but to buy the best example, usually possible at a specialized pottery show from a reputable dealer with reasonable prices. That way you can examine your purchase and make sure you are getting what you pay for and not wasting your time and money on a bargain that isn't.

In order of popularity, the basic Catalina glazes are Catalina Blue (matt), which is described as being between an Alice and a cobalt blue, Descanso Green (matt), Toyon Red (matt), a cherry-orange named after the berries found on the Island, Mandarin or "Manchu" Yellow (gloss), Turquoise Blue (gloss), and Ivory or White (matt). The scarce high gloss glazes are Monterey Brown, which has been described as a cup of coffee with cream poured over it, and was designed as a go-along for Monterey furniture,

and Seafoam, a greenish-blue. Both have highly varying ranges of tones and shades that sometimes cause confusion. The hardest to find glaze colors on pottery are Teal (gloss), Obsidian Black (gloss), and a dark mottled cobalt. Catalina used a brown underglaze slip on many pieces that, when fired, showed through the glaze color in a "burn" of brown or greenish hue. This is a desirable effect but it sometimes causes people to think that it's the "red clay" showing through. A common form in a rare color will not bring a great price, but a rare form in a rare color can. The blended glaze pricing depends totally on the aesthetics of any given piece.

Glazes on the later Deco line (which includes Starlight, Rope, and some crossover pieces) produced in 1936 used at least some of the original glaze colors such as Turquoise and Toyon Red. Mandarin Yellow changed its name but not its hue and followed the furniture trends by becoming "Colonial Yellow." New glazes added were "satin finish" colors such as Pearly White, Coral Island (peach), Powder Blue, and a two-tone blue and white finish. Although numerous examples can be found in the Deco line it was produced for a very short period of time just prior to the plant's closing.

Cowboy hat ashtrays. All glaze colors but black. 6" x 5" plus or minus. All signed "Catalina" or "Catalina Island." Remember, several other California potteries sold almost identical-looking hats. $175 - $325. *Courtesy of Allan & Laurie Carter.*

Variety of handled vases. Monterey Brown high gloss glaze. Ranging from 15" to 7". NP. *Courtesy of John Phelps.*

Cigar humidor with lid. Black glaze with gold paint underglaze. Bucking Bronco design. 6" tall. NP. *Courtesy of Steven Hoefs.*

Seafoam high gloss glaze, color variations from brownish blue to lighter green. NP. *Courtesy of Jerry Kunz.*

Leaf candelabra showing "burn" on red glaze. White clay, one of a pair. *Courtesy of Jerry Kunz.*

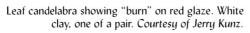

Marks

The only truly "early" marks for Catalina are the ink stamps found on early blended glaze pieces. Other ink stamps used on Island pieces include a smaller circular version seen on the inside of some lamps and bud vases, as well as on the foot of some Catalina Bears, and a semicircular stamp used on an early felt tile backing and one table lamp. Other than the late Deco design vases, which sometimes include numbers, most of the other pottery marks were used throughout the life of the company and cannot be accurately used for dating. A sampling of marks are shown here. All say "Catalina Island," "Catalina Isle," or simply "Catalina," some might even say "Catalina Island Pottery." Most of the marks were "in mold," including many that look "hand-inscribed," some were iron or hand "stamped." The method of signature does *not* affect the price, but of course some beginning collectors do feel more secure with marked pieces. Many items are unmarked, particularly the lamps and smaller pieces such as figurines. There were many different stickers that were used as well, a few are shown here. The jury's still out on a purple and silver sticker that says "Souvenir of Catalina Island" and has surfaced on pieces believed to have been made by Caliente Pottery, even though sold on the Island.

This book focuses on Island made pottery only, *not* pottery made by Gladding McBean from 1937 to 1942 after they purchased the Catalina name. Gladding McBean made exact duplicates of some items from Island molds as well as creating many distinctive artware and dinnerware lines for the six years leading up to World War II. Many people collect both but it is important to know the difference. Gladding McBean-made Catalina wares are marked "Catalina Pottery" and often include a "Made in U.S.A." ink stamp. There is a shortcut terminology collector's use that is handy to know. All Gladding McBean Catalina is called "pottery' and all Island made wares are called "Island", as in "Is that vase "pottery" or Island?"

A knowledge of glazes and forms is required to accurately identify Catalina pieces. There are many reproduction tiles on the market that are exact duplicates of historic Catalina tiles. They are usually lightweight, thinner, and unmarked. Nothing beats holding and examining a tile to determine its authenticity. One of the difficulties in buying on the Internet (forgetting hidden damage, repairs, or fakes) is that it is very difficult to see those glazes accurately. Given low quality or fuzzy digital images, *and* computer enhancements, even an amateur can easily keep damage out of view. Padre, Poxon, Tudor, Caliente, and Gladding McBean are among the many potteries who made quite similar, sometimes identical pieces. Buying from a reputable source that guarantees condition and maker is essential.

Mark from Trojan teapot, "Catalina Island" in unique thin block letters. This same signature is seen on early experimental bulbous vases. Possibly an early or transitional mark. *Courtesy of Jerry Kunz.*

"Catalina" in block letters.

"Catalina Island," with Catalina curved in a half oval.

"Catalina Island" signature in script. This was an in mold mark.

Another in mold mark, "Catalina."

Black and silver paper label, "Avalonware." This is the only place you'll see "Catalina Pottery" on an Island piece. From the rarely seen "Embossed Beer Stein."

"Catalina Island" signature.

"Catalina" paper label.

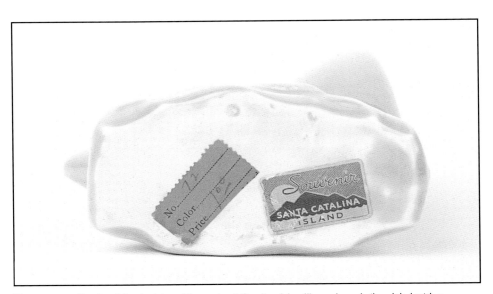

Not a proven Catalina Island sticker. "Souvenir of Catalina Island" purple and silver label with a mountain. Sometimes found on non-Island made wares by Caliente Pottery.

It's a vase. It's a pitcher. It's three designs in one! All Catalina Island. Turquoise, blue, and green glazes. 6" high. NP. *Courtesy of Jerry Kunz.*

Catalina blue fan vase & Padre green fan vase. 9" & 6". Note similar form and glazes. Hard to tell apart from a photo. $250 & $50. *Courtesy of Carole Coates.*

Catalina Island Pottery

Patio Pottery
Color in the Garden

Patio pottery was hot in the late 1920s. D.M. Renton's focus turned to expanding Catalina's garden ware line, very popular because of Southern California's year 'round outdoor life-style. He toured mainland gardens and homes in October and November of 1929 to research Spanish style homes, gardens, and their accessories. He visited Harold Lloyd's "Greenacres" estate, which had over 6,000 of these pots alone. He also went to the Santa Barbara Biltmore, surveyed the Spanish style architecture, and must have admired the beautiful Gladding McBean tile ship murals, stair risers, and archways, all done in colorful decorative tiles. By November of 1929, D.M. stated emphatically "we are making wonderful pottery now." (Wrigley-Renton correspondence)

Flower pots of assorted colors and sizes. NP.
Courtesy of Carole Coates.

A display of flower pots on a Catalina checkerboard table. Green and unglazed pots. NP. *Courtesy of Carole Coates.*

Selection of flower pots: blue, green, red, and Monterey Brown. 5 7/8" to 3". NP. *Courtesy of Carole Coates.*

Flower pots of assorted colors and sizes. $125 - $175. *Courtesy of Carole Coates.*

Various flower pots. Descanso Green. 6 3/8" to 3". $95 - $175. *Courtesy of Allan & Laurie Carter.*

Cactus bowl. Red glaze, smallest of two sizes. 8" across. $125. *Courtesy of Jerry Kunz.*

Ringed flower pot in original iron holder with ivy motif. White. Pot: $65. Holder: $150. *Courtesy of Carole Coates.*

Checkerboard table with two ringed flower pots. Red glaze pots. *Courtesy of Carole Coates.*

Opposite page
Left: Ringed flowerpot in original Island-made wooden stand. Red glaze. 30" high in stand. $650. *Courtesy of Carole Coates.*

Right: Tripod planter, four colors. Hard to find. 3" high. $150. *Courtesy of Jerry Kunz.*

Tile fountain utilizing early "wavy" tiles and plain field tiles. Installed in 1930. *Courtesy of Dr. Staff.*

Two backgammon tile planters, concrete interiors. One with border tile at base. 14" is six sided & 10 1/2" is four sided. $950 & $550. *Courtesy of Carole Coates.*

Floral decorative tile planter box. Rarely seen 12" tiles are otherwise only found on single bird motif tiles at the Isthmus and in some private homes. Note: Reproduction tiles are made in this and many other Catalina styles and sizes. NP. *Courtesy of Carole Coates.*

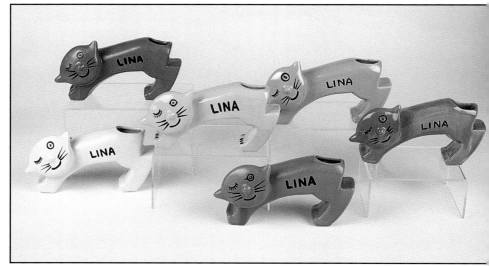

'Lina (as in Cat o 'lina) cactus planters, six colors. 3" high x 7" long. $200 - $500+. *Courtesy of Jerry Kunz.*

Black 'Lina cactus planter (as in Cat o lina) with gold paint. NP. *Courtesy of Steven Hoefs.*

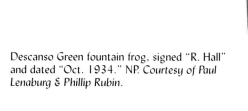

Descanso Green fountain frog, signed "R. Hall" and dated "Oct. 1934." NP. *Courtesy of Paul Lenaburg & Phillip Rubin.*

Garden or entry pot. Hard to find shape and size, especially undamaged. 13" high, 12" across at widest point. Green glaze. $475+. *Courtesy of Carole Coates.*

Oil jar in original Island-made wooden stand. Red glaze. 26" high in stand. $1,800. *Courtesy of Carole Coates.*

Oil jar in original Island-made iron stand. Red glaze. 28" high in stand. $2,000 with stand. *Courtesy of Carole Coates.*

Oil jar in earliest original iron holder. Green glaze. 17" high, jar only. $2,200 with stand. *Courtesy of Allan & Laurie Carter.*

Tall handled urn, used for gardens and entry halls. Blue glaze, very hard to find form. 22" tall. $3,000+. *Courtesy of Carole Coates.*

Large handled urn. Difficult to find without damage. Green gla... 18" tall. $2,000. *Courtesy of Carole Coat...*

Oil jar, blue glaze. 17" high. $1,200+. *Courtesy of Carole Coates.*

Around the House
Colors of the Island

In 1930, The Catalina Clay Products Company came into being as a separate entity focused on pottery for home, garden, and table. It was called the pottery "plant." The Tile Factory, the "factory" of course, continued its building material production and geared up its decorative tile production during this period. On the Island, shops in the Atwater Arcade, The Island Villas, the Casino Way Pottery Shop, and the Bird Park sold Catalina pottery and tile.

Mr. Virgil Haldeman officially worked with Catalina from June 1930 until 1933. Haldeman was a "glaze man" with an experienced background and a fine reputation. It was during this productive period that Catalina began to make a wide array of vases and an expanded house wares line. The name "Catalinaware" and "Avalon-ware" began to be used in 1932 along with a blitz of publicity and "news" articles. Haldeman's arrival also coincided with an increased production and variety of design in tile. Whether this is related to his influence or to the arrival of Mr. John Wilde in 1931 (see page 128) is not known — nor is Haldeman's contribution to developing Catalina's classic glaze colors. He is credited with developing later glazes that were used on the "Starlight" and "Rope" dinnerware lines, as well as some of the later Deco line vases that were produced after his official tenure at Catalina. The Avalon newspaper makes mention of many "Haldeman's" living there during the 1930s, some noted as sports fishermen and avid boaters. Given the "small world" connections of the Island it would not be surprising if these people were family members, and provided additional reasons for Mr. Haldeman to "consult" with Catalina in it's remaining years. Haldeman first came to California in 1926 after earning his degree as a ceramic engineer at the University of Illinois in 1923. He was employed by California Clay Products Company, known as CALCO, in 1926. It is not known if his arrival overlapped with another University of Illinois attendee, Rufus Keeler, prior to Keeler's departure from CALCO, but it is certainly another interesting coincidence connecting them both to Catalina.

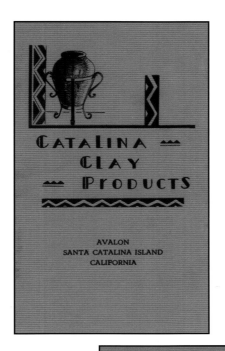

Early "Catalina Clay Products" brochure, circa 1931. Shows Moorish plate, oil jar in early holder, Spanish pots, and others. *Courtesy of Catalina Island Museum.*

An invoice from Catalina Clay Products from the 1930s. *Courtesy of the Malcolm J. Renton Collection.*

Popular Science Magazine, May 1932.

Vases

Most of Catalina's vase designs and forms are original to the pottery even though at the time it was perfectly acceptable to copy from classic periods. Influences range from Arts and Crafts and Art Deco to Spanish and Native American. Handled, ringed, fluted, raised design, and smooth forms were made in a large variety of styles, whether slip cast, molded, or hand thrown. Some forms were only made in the early years and others were made throughout the life of the pottery. Catalina collectors never know what exciting items might pop up next and vases certainly are one area where experimental forms are regularly found. Catalina combined practicality and beauty in this popular item and, even with extremely expensive pieces, collectors today don't hesitate to enjoy using them for, guess what? Flowers.

CATALINAWARE

IT has been but recently that the extensive deposits of many fine clays, unknown for centuries, have been found in the hills and canyons of Catalina Island. These clays, similar to those found in Egypt deposited by the Nile, have led to the establishment of the oldest of crafts and arts, that of hand-made and hand-decorated pottery and tile, at Avalon. One especially rare clay at Catalina is found at the bottom of Echo Lake which is situated near the summit of one of the highest mountains on the Island, Mount Black Jack. This is a very plastic clay, rich in kaolin, which lends itself to the molding of the finest pottery and tile. Silicas and aluminas, also found on the Island, burn into the most beautiful glazes, to which the mineral oxides known to the Indians lend a vividness of coloring and a brilliant metallic luster that is distinctive to the Catalina products.

The degree of hardness to which the pottery products are brought is indicated by their resonance—they give forth beautiful musical tones similar to those made by the pottery manufactured from the clay secured in Devonshire, England.

It is in the chronicles of Father Torquemada, who accompanied the Spanish explorer Viscaíno upon his trips in the capacity of historian, that a graphic picture is drawn of the type of "white" Indians who inhabited Catalina Island and bartered with the mainland Indians, exchanging great urns, bowls and ollas of stone which they tediously chiseled with their crude implements, for baskets and pottery. Little did the island Indians dream that close at hand upon beautiful Catalina, their own place of residence, were finer clays than those to which their brothers of the mainland had access. On the Island were silicas for glazes and mineral oxides for colorings from which the early Catalina inhabitants could have made pottery of a beauty far excelling that for which they bartered. The vivid red and yellow ochres found on the Island were used by the Catalina Indians only as a means of personal adornment and to paint the symbols of the sun and moon and other objects which struck their fancy or which were a part of their religious ceremonies.

Just recently it was discovered that the island clay lends itself admirably to the production of a very high grade of pottery and tile and immediately when samples were made up, it was also discovered that the thousands of people who visited the Island each year welcomed the pottery and tile as affording an opportunity to take away a very attractive souvenir of the beautiful Magic Isle.

At Pebbly Beach, the eastern terminus of the Avalon Board walk, about three-quarters of a mile from town, is situated the Catalina Pottery and Tile Plant. Here hundreds of craftsmen and artists are busily engaged in transforming bits of the Magic Isle into beautiful objects of ornament and utility. A wide variety of useful and attract-

ive articles are manufactured and the industry has grown rapidly until now not only is a vast quantity produced but a full line of the products has been placed on sale in all of the leading stores throughout Southern California and elsewhere. Consignments have been made to dealers at remote points including many of the leading cities of the U. S. A. A most attractive display sample shop is maintained on Olvera Street in Los Angeles and there are several shops in Avalon. Hundreds of visitors to the Island order pottery to be shipped to their home address or to friends and relatives as gifts.

In addition to a wide range in size, shape and purpose, the pottery comes in a variety of colors including beautiful Catalina Blue, Toyon Red, Descanso Green, Obsidian Black, Manchu Yellow, etc. Many pieces of pottery are hand-decorated by native Catalina girls trained in the art of applying the varied colored glazes. Much of the beauty and quality of Catalina tile and pottery is due to the unusually high temperatures at which the Island clays can be burned and the great care with which only perfect pieces are selected.

Many of the decorative motifs of Catalina pottery and tile are suggested by subjects typical of the Island—leaping swordfish, gossamer-winged flying fish, exotic and brilliantly plumaged birds of the Catalina Bird Park, the vivid poinsettias that are found on the Island, Spanish galleons and conventionalized patterns of the Alta California influence.

Catalina tables with their decorative tile tops are an especially attractive product. The selection of pottery products is so extensive as to meet the desires of any taste or requirement; lamps of various sizes and shapes completely wired for electricity, vases, flower pots, jardinieres, bowls, plates, cups and saucers, candle sticks, cigar jars, ash trays, condiment dishes; in fact so many articles of Catalina pottery are available that selection is practically unlimited.

CATALINAWARE

GR-50M. 6-33

"Catalinaware." Catalina Island Pottery and Tile sales brochure. 3 views. *Courtesy of Allan and Laurie Carter*

Left: Dog-eared vase. Very hard to find form. Blue glaze. 14". $1,800. *Courtesy of Carole Coates.*

Right: Variety of handled vases. Monterey Brown glaze. Ranging from 15" to 7". NP. *Courtesy of John Phelps.*

Bottom right: "Step" vases. 5" high. Turquoise, white, red, and green. Note that this form was copied in a smaller form by other California potteries. $300+. *Courtesy of Carole Coates.*

Two handled vase. Green glaze. Similar form found in other California potteries. 5" high. $375. *Courtesy of Carole Coates.*

Two handled urn. Turquoise glaze. Most commonly found of the large 2 handled vases. Also appears in table lamp form, sometimes with a glazed factory hole. 15" tall. $950. *Courtesy of Jerry Kunz.*

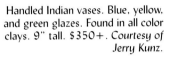

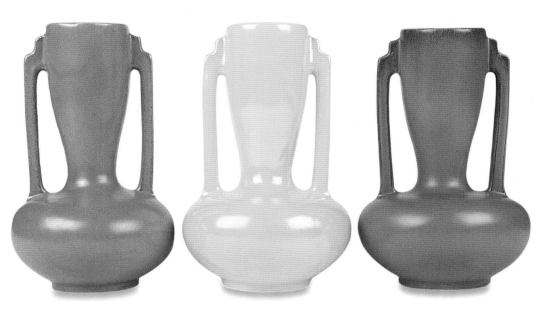

Handled Indian vases. Blue, yellow, and green glazes. Found in all color clays. 9" tall. $350+. *Courtesy of Jerry Kunz.*

"Trophy" floor vases, with and without handles. Red and blue glazes. 15" tall. This vase comes in many sizes down to a 7" size. $1,200 and $900. *Courtesy of Jerry Kunz*

"Trophy" vases, three sizes. Blue, green, and red. Often inscribed on special occasions such as boat races and fishing contests. Sometimes found converted to a lamp form. Not rare, but makes a nice display in varying heights. 15", 11", and 7". $750, $550, $350. *Courtesy of Jerry Kunz.*

Raised design floral vases. Very hard to find. Blue glaze. 11" and 7" tall. $1,000+ and $750+. *Courtesy of Steven Hoefs.*

Cherry Tree with Birds. Raised design vase. Descanso Green. 10". $1,000. *Courtesy of Jerry Kunz.*

Same vases, different view.

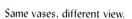

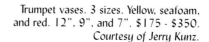

Indian vases. Raised design. Blue and orange glazes. 4" and 3" high. $750+, $450. *Courtesy of Carole Coates.*

Trumpet vases. 3 sizes. Yellow, seafoam, and red. 12", 9", and 7". $175 - $350. *Courtesy of Jerry Kunz.*

Floral line vases. Seafoam, red, blue, and white. Showing 4 of the 5 sizes made. 13", 11", 8", & 6". $150 - $550. Courtesy of Jerry Kunz.

an vase. Turquoise and red glaze. 9", the smaller of 2 sizes. $200 +, $325. Courtesy of Jerry Kunz.

Assortment of Catalina Blue vases. Courtesy of Carole Coates.

Floral line vases. Largest and smallest sizes. Seafoam & blue. This form is common, yet popular, and was sold to florists throughout the country. 13" high to 6" high. $150 - $550+. Courtesy of Jerry Kunz.

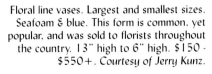

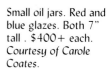

Small oil jars. Red and blue glazes. Both 7" tall . $400+ each. *Courtesy of Carole Coates.*

Two mid-sized floral line vases. Red and blue glazes. $350 - $150. *Courtesy of Carole Coates.*

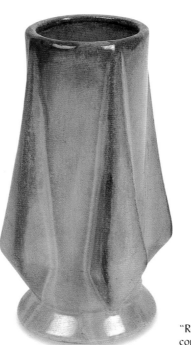

Large experimental pot/vase. Monterey Brown, signed "Catalina." 10" tall with 5" opening. NP. *Courtesy of John Phelps.*

Same jars, different view.

"Rocket" vase. Monterey Brown glaze. 6" tall. Note that this form was copied by other California potteries. $400. *Courtesy of Carole Coates.*

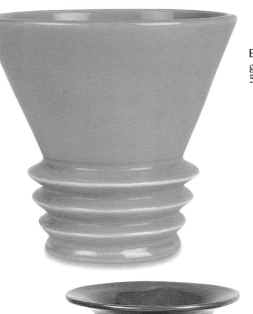

Early Deco vase. Hard to find form. Turquoise glaze. Marked "Catalina Island" and "325". 5" high. $395+. *Courtesy of Steven Hoefs.*

Assortment of ringed vases. Footed and bulbous vases are hard to find forms. Blue glaze. 8", 8", and 5". Left: $500. Right: $650+. Center: $250. *Courtesy of Carole Coates.*

Tapered, bud, and rocket vases. All in scarce black glaze. Bud vase has gold paint under glaze. 6" to 4". NP. *Courtesy of Jerry Kunz.*

Grouping of 4 vases in assorted shapes and sizes for perspective. Red glaze. *Courtesy of Carole Coates.*

Ringed experimental vase. Hand thrown, unmarked, but with an unmistakable clay and a Toyon Red glaze. 12". NP. *Courtesy of Paul Lenaburg & Phillip Rubin.*

Bud vase with rare gold painted rings. Red glaze. 4" high. $175. *Courtesy of Carole Coates.*

Cornucopia bud vase. Green. 5" high. $400. *Courtesy of Carole Coates.*

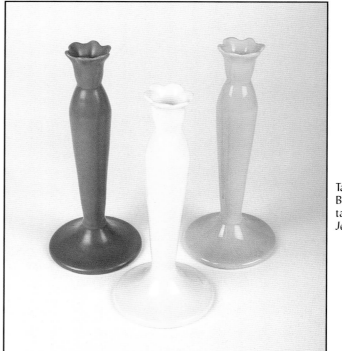

Tall bud vases. Fluted tops. Blue, yellow, and white. 8" tall. $225 each. *Courtesy of Jerry Kunz.*

Two handled urn. All brown under glaze, possibly burnt in kiln. 15" high. $450. *Courtesy of Carole Coates.*

Very large clamshell bowl. Blue glaze. Common in Gladding McBean, only a few have been seen in Island ware. Unmarked. 15" across. $1,000+. *Courtesy of Steven Hoefs.*

Nautilus shell. Green glaze. 6" tall x 8 1/2" across. $650. *Courtesy of Steven Hoefs.*

Shell table vase. Same form as wall pocket, but without a glazed hole. 9" long, red. $350. *Courtesy of Carole Coates.*

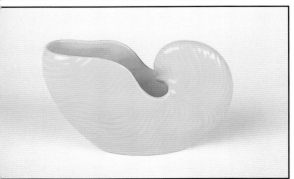

Nautilus shell "vase." Yellow glaze. 8" long. $650. *Courtesy of Jerry Kunz.*

A bountiful display of Catalina vases. *Courtesy of Jerry Kunz.*

Lamps

Catalina lamps provided both color and light in one easy package. Small little scout lamps and large majestic urns were made with either original iron fixtures or hand-painted parchment shades laced with Catalina goatskin. The lamps were made in a variety of forms and sizes. Many are not marked, since the small rims didn't lend themselves to it. Most of the vase forms are hollow-based and are glazed both inside and out. Some vases were later converted into lamp form and have drilled holes, a few lamps were made out of vase forms and have hardware original to the factory; however, in order to be considered a "real" lamp most purists insist on a factory glazed hole. A knowledge of form, clay, and glaze are necessary for proper identification of unmarked pieces.

Cactus table lamp. Raised design. Teal glaze. Rarest of the rare. Contemporary shade. Base height 12". $3,000+. Courtesy of Steven Hoefs.

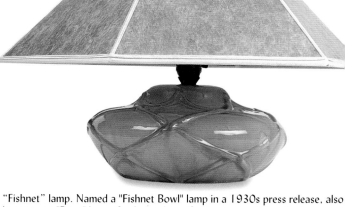

"Fishnet" lamp. Named a "Fishnet Bowl" lamp in a 1930s press release, also known as a "Rope" lamp. Seafoam glaze. Contemporary Mica shade. $2,000+. Courtesy of Carole Coates.

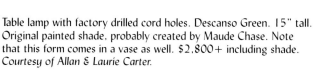

Table lamp with factory drilled cord holes. Descanso Green. 15" tall. Original painted shade, probably created by Maude Chase. Note that this form comes in a vase as well. $2,800+ including shade. Courtesy of Allan & Laurie Carter.

"Fishnet" lamp without shade. Green glaze. $1,500. Courtesy of Carole Coates.

Table lamp with "Elephant Trunk" handles. 8". Catalina Blue. Hardly seen form. New Mexicana style shade. $2,500+. Courtesy of Allan & Laurie Carter.

Turban lamp. Similar to the "Fishnet" form but without a net. Blue glaze. Contemporary shade. $1,200. *Courtesy of Carole Coates.*

Table lamp with new skin shade. Blue glaze. More commonly found form. $1,000. *Courtesy of Carole Coates.*

Table lamp with tapered "foot." Mica shade. Green glaze. 9". $2,800. *Courtesy of Jerry Kunz.*

"Ball" shaped lamp. Uncommon form. Red glaze. Contemporary custom printed shade painted by Joni LaGoy of Bisbee, Arizona, as are most of the newer shades pictured. $1,500. *Courtesy of Carole Coates.*

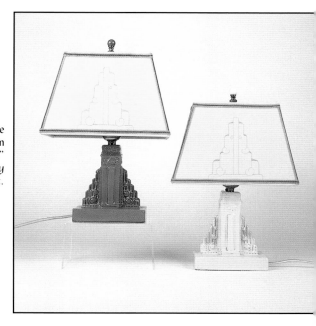

Scout lamp with a brass chimney holder. 5" high base. Red glaze. $450. Courtesy of Carole Coates.

Table lamps. Custom contemporary shades. Blue glaze. Not often seen. Base height 10" & 8". $2,800+. Courtesy of Steven Hoefs.

Monument lamps. 6" high. Blue and white. With new custom shades. Signed "Catalina." $1,000+ each. Courtesy of Jerry Kunz.

Bulbous lamp. Black glaze. The ceramic body was used in a vase form as well. This example has a factory glazed electric cord hole & lamp hardware that proves this piece was intended to be used as a lamp rather than a vase. 6". $750. Courtesy of Carole Coates.

Yellow handled scout lamp. Original painted metal shade. $850. *Courtesy of Paul Lenaburg & Phillip Rubin.*

Three Scout lamps. Black, red, and green glazed. 5" hexagonal base. Custard cup base is 3" to bulb. Original metal shades and "lantern" shaped bulbs. $600+. *Courtesy of Carole Coates.*

Three Scout lamps. With chimney and new reproduction shades. 4" & 3" bases. Yellow, red, and blue. $500+. *Courtesy of Carole Coates.*

Scout lamp. Green glaze with plate backing. $550. *Courtesy of Allan & Laurie Carter.*

Various lamps in different colors. It might be hard to tell but these lamps are very small, ranging from 3"
to 5" across.

Iron lamp base with tile. $550.

Bookends

Bookends were one of the first items made by the pottery and as they evolved into more sophisticated forms they continued to be very popular. It is believed that some later Deco style bookends were made as well. The early ones are solid and very heavy, made of red brick type clay, and still show a strong Arts and Crafts influence. All are considered hard to find, especially in a pair and undamaged, but the Monks are the most often found, followed by Frogs. All other forms are exceedingly rare. The ship bookends shown here comprise the only pair currently known to exist. There have been "sightings" of other unusual bookends including Lion's Heads, Cacti, and others that we hope to include in the next revision of this book.

Monk bookends. Blue glaze. Signed "Catalina". Very heavy. Similar to Malibu and Gladding McBean. $2,000. *Courtesy of Jerry Kunz.*

Monk bookends. Monterey Brown. They face in different directions to make a pair. 5" tall x 4" across. $2,500+. *Courtesy of John Phelps.*

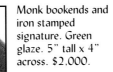

Monk bookends and iron stamped signature. Green glaze. 5" tall x 4" across. $2,000.

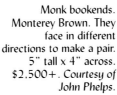

Frog bookends and bottom mark. Green glaze. 4" long x 4" high. Green. $2,500+. *Courtesy of Carole Coates.*

Ship bookends. Green glaze. 4 1/2" high, 3 1/2" base. Sticker on bottom says "Doug S. Loud". NP. *Courtesy of Catalina Island Museum.*

Star tile bookends. In iron holders. 3 5/8" tiles. $750. *Courtesy of Carole Coates.*

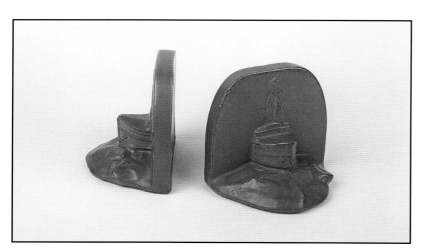

Another view of Ship bookends.

Casino humidor. Made as special gifts for employees. Usually signed with the first name and last initial of a plant worker. Monterey Brown. 5" tall x 4" across. NP.

Smoking Sets

Made throughout the life of the pottery, smoking accessories were one of the most fanciful and original lines yet, especially since "everybody" smoked. These novelty items are much sought after today, although it's doubtful that any of these pricey ashtrays would risk a cigarette burn. This inventive line enabled every Island visitor to do what Mr. Wrigley hoped they would, "take home a piece of Catalina" with them. Items were molded or slip-cast, and are found primarily in white clay. Surely the more refined white clays gave better results on the slip cast pieces. Many novelties were "cold-painted" in playful ways. This does increase the kitsch factor but to find a piece with even peeling original paint is always considered a plus.

Considered authentic in the 1930s, today images of "peons" and "Sleeping Mexicans" are thought of as being quaint or naïve, some as downright stereotypical. Obviously they were patronizing to many Latinos of that era. In a recollection from Olvera Street, a young girl painting a mural of a "Sleepy Mexican" on a wall in the 1930s is told by her offended uncle to redo it. "I want that Mexican awake by tomorrow," he said. Even the romantic images were of an imaginary time, such as the stunning one-of-a-kind figure by Bud Upton of a kneeling Spanish man on the cover of Steven Hoef's Catalina book. Collectors of California made "Mexicana" from that era appreciate the images with the knowledge and perspective of the tremendous contributions of Mexico in general and Latinos in particular to the arts in California.

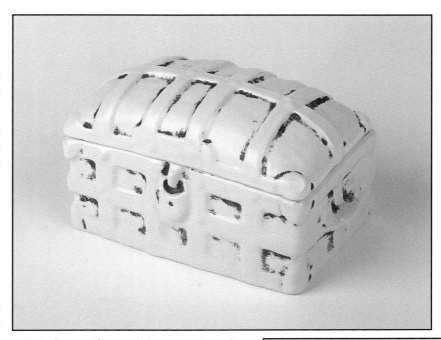

White Treasure Chest with faux rust paint and bottom price tag. $2,000+. Courtesy of Paul Lenaburg & Phillip Rubin.

Treasure Chest box. Blue glaze. 3 5/8" high, 6" long. Designed by "Bud" Upton. $2,000+. Courtesy of Carole Coates.

Treasure Chest mark, with paper price tag sticker.

Cigar humidor and various cigarette boxes. Blue and white glazes. Courtesy of Carole Coates.

Cigar humidor with lid. Black glaze with gold paint under glaze. Bucking Bronco design. 6" tall. NP. *Courtesy of Steven Hoefs.*

Detail of ashtray holder showing the four ashtrays that came in the set.

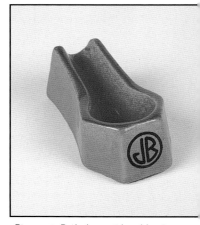

Pipe rest. Red glaze with cold paint monogram. 4" long. *Courtesy of Jerry Kunz.*

Ashtray holder with raised Deco flower detail. Black glaze with gold paint given as a trophy gift. NP.

DARSIE L. DARSIE
SPORTS WRITER
4TH ANNUAL CATALINA
WOMEN'S GOLF TOURNAMENT
MAY 1932

Horse head cigarette box. Green glaze is unusual for this form. 3" tall. $175 in a typical glaze. $300+ here. *Courtesy of Steven Hoefs.*

Pipe rest with vintage Catalina lighter. Blue and seafoam. 4" long. $150. *Courtesy of Carole Coates.*

Square ashtray set (4) and humidor with lid in raised bird motif. Note that all sides show different birds. 3" & 4" high. Monterey Brown and red. $450+, $350. *Courtesy of Jerry Kunz and Carole Coates.*

Black Bear "Cub" made in honor of Wrigley's beloved Chicago Cubs baseball team. $850+. *Courtesy of Steven Hoefs.*

Round cigarette humidor with lid and ashtray holder with four handled ashtrays. Yellow and blue. Raised Deco flowers design. 4" and 3" tall. $400 and $350. *Courtesy of Jerry Kunz.*

Bear figurine cigarette holder. Monterey Brown. Original cold paint. $650+. NP. *Courtesy of Larry Harris.*

Bear figurine cigarette holder's ink stamp on foot.

Baseball ashtray &
cigarette holder. Green
glaze. 3". NP. *Courtesy
of Steven Hoefs.*

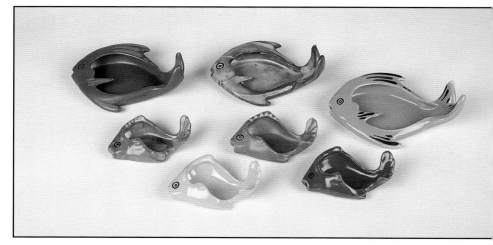

School of Catalina Fish ashtrays. Cold paint. 4" and 6". $125 - $225. *Courtesy of Jerry Kunz.*

Baseball Mitt. Monterey
Brown glaze. 4" across.
NP. *Courtesy of Steven
Hoefs.*

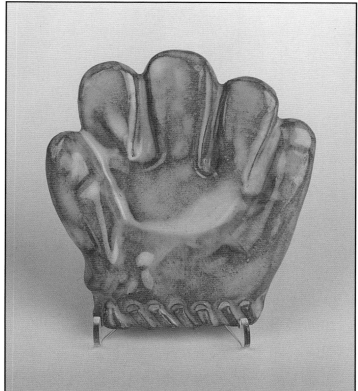

Starfish ashtrays. Blue, turquoise, white, and green. 5" long. $225. *Courtesy of Jerry Kunz.*

Seal ashtray with sticker. Front reads "Catalina". Green glaze. $450. *Courtesy of Allan & Laurie Carter.*

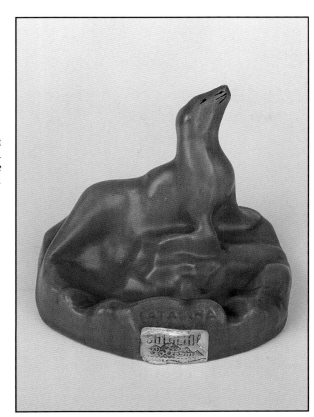

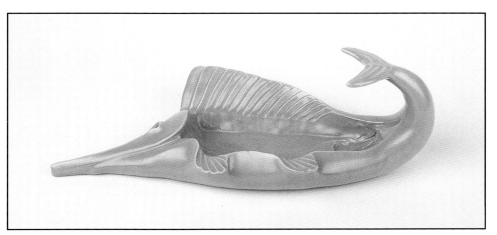

Swordfish ashtray, hand formed. Unusual powder blue glaze. Not marked. The tail dips in just as the fish ashtray's does. It is possible this was an off-hours project, many of which were very creative. 14 1/4" long, 6 1/2" wide. NP. *Courtesy of Steven Hoefs.*

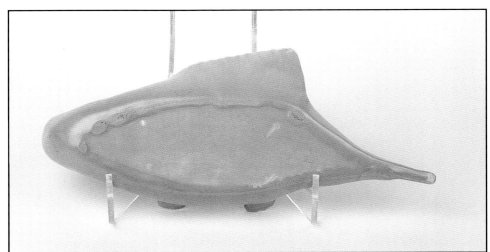

Bottom of Swordfish ashtray.

Shell ashtrays. Green, Monterey Brown, blue, and yellow. Nesting. 5 1/4" long, 4 1/4" across. This is the larger of two sizes made. $95 - $125. *Courtesy of Carole Coates.*

Figural ashtrays. "Goofyfoot Goat" in blue. Reclining Goat in Monterey Brown, Seal in turquoise, and Bear in Monterey Brown. 4" to 3" tall. $350 to $850. *Courtesy of Jerry Kunz.*

Siesta ashtray and Mexican chalk version (a copy of Catalina's, but in chalk). Green glaze. 7" across at widest point. $500+ and $30. *Courtesy of Carole Coates.*

Cowboy advertising hat. "Pendolinos" in mold on crown. Monterey Brown glaze. $275. *Courtesy of Allan & Laurie Carter.*

Five cowboy hat ashtrays in various colors.

Large ashtray with four "tabs." Turquoise. 9 1/2".
$195. *Courtesy of Bob and Barbara Crow.*

Chimes Tower clock. Very few
made. Turquoise glaze on white
clay. 7 3/4" tall x 5 1/2". NP.
Courtesy of Steven Hoefs.

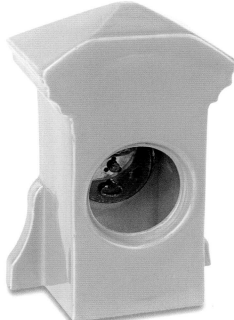

Chimes Tower back view.

Octagonal ashtrays, also known as "pin" trays. 3" and 2 5/8". Hard to find in the smallest size. Green and
Monterey Brown. $150+, $125. *Courtesy of Jerry Kunz.*

Other Novelties: A Touch of Color

Catalina was especially inventive when it came to household items. Other potteries made wall pockets, but Catalina's had a raised basket weave design, and looked almost like slippers. Clocks in the shape of the Chimes Tower and other unusual pieces showed a fanciful touch while retaining a totally unique Island theme. Figurines provided a decorative splash of color on the shelf or table, but figural shapes were also incorporated into practical table and dinnerware items such as salt and pepper shakers, carafe lids and flower frogs. Even buttons and belt buckles were molded and glazed for that "Catalina" accent on sweaters and jackets.

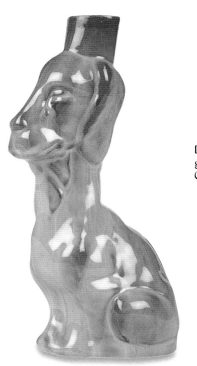

Dog candleholder. Monterey Brown glaze. Very unusual form. Unsigned. NP. *Courtesy of Jerry Kunz.*

Novelty Cats. Cold painted faces. One is marked. Blue and white. 4 3/8". $500. *Courtesy of Allan & Laurie Carter.*

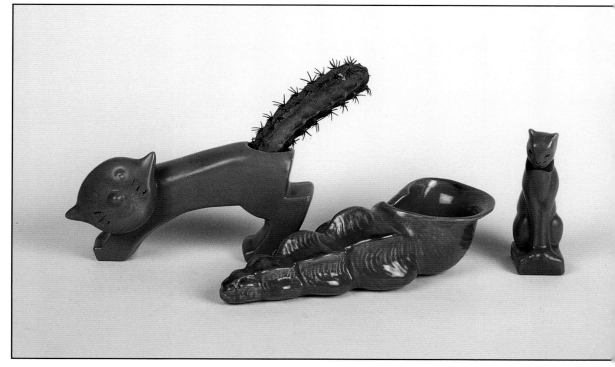

Size perspective on 'Lina, Shell vase, and Novelty Cat.

Covered box with finial. May be one of a kind. Green glaze. 1" high. NP. *Courtesy of Steven Hoefs.*

Basket weave wall pockets. Red and white. 9" and 7" sizes only. $250+, $350. *Courtesy of Jerry Kunz.*

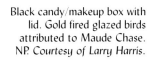

Black candy/makeup box with lid. Gold fired glazed birds attributed to Maude Chase. NP. *Courtesy of Larry Harris.*

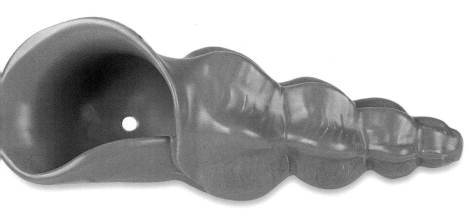

Shell wall pocket. Blue glaze. Glazed hole for hanging. (This piece is also found in a vase form.) 8" long. $350. *Courtesy of Jerry Kunz.*

Another view of black candy box. *Courtesy of Larry Harris.*

Handled basket. Green glaze. Unmarked. 6". NP. *Courtesy of Steven Hoefs.*

Green button and belt buckle set. Sewn on original paper backing "made on Catalina Island". NP. *Courtesy of Steven Hoefs.*

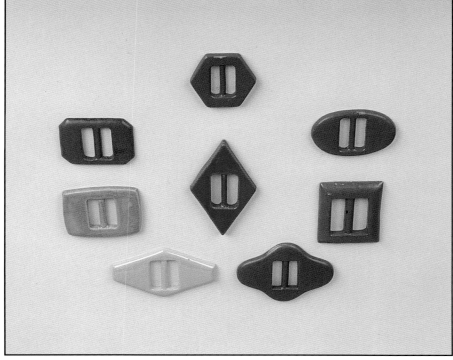

Belt buckles. Various glazes. 2" to 3". $200 – $300 each. *Courtesy of Steven Hoefs.*

Detail of button set.

Catalina Lucie

Lucie Watkins worked in the Atwater Arcade and hand formed many unique pieces, including candlesticks and centerpiece bowls (sometimes matching), bookends, wall pockets, and, more rarely, novelties and lamps with applied flowers. The majority of her work was done with a floral theme and used pastel glazes unlike the typical Catalina colors; but, whimsical swordfish and flying fish items have surfaced as well. Her Island pieces are signed "Catalina Lucie." She continued her work for many years on the mainland in her own studio and signed these pieces, "Lucie" and "Made in California."

Lamp with decorative hand applied flowers. Yellow glaze. Attributed to Lucie Watkins. 9 3/4" high. $2,000. *Courtesy of Bob & Barbara Crow.*

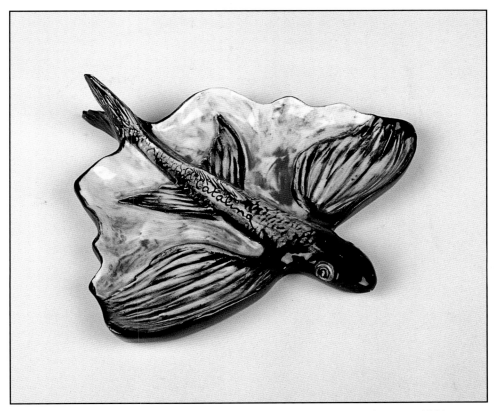

Flying Fish ashtray. Signed "Made on Catalina Island. Original design Lucie". 8" across. $350. *Courtesy of Jerry Kunz.*

Back of Flying Fish ashtray.

Decorative Plates
Island Imagery

A unique setting created a unique art on Catalina Island. No other California pottery made such a wide array of distinctive designs and original art that at the same time was so remarkably reflective of California's life-style. There are four main categories of decorative plates: glazed, raised design, hand painted, and glaze "painted." They are all found in a dazzling choice of colors and designs. Many believe these wares to be the epitome of Catalina Island "style." It's not known who deserves the credit for designing either these or all but one of the similarly designed pictorial tile murals but it seems likely that the ideas, if not the execution, came from the artists in residence who created the hand painted plates. Most of the plates were designed to be used as wall decorations and many have pre-pierced holes for a hanging wire, while some were intended to double as either "fruit plates" or to be displayed in a china cabinet.

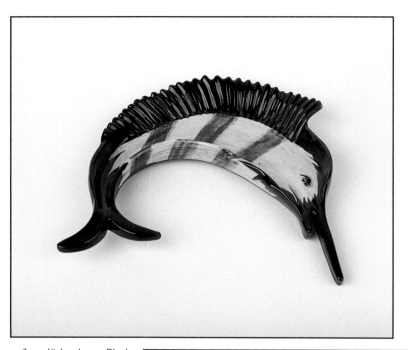

Swordfish ashtray. Black glazed fins. Signed "Catalina Lucie". 7" long. NP. Courtesy of Catalina Island Museum.

Various floral wall pockets. Lucille Watkins. Signed "Made in California. Lucie". $150 to $350. Courtesy of Jerry Kunz.

"Seahorse" glazed wall plates. Cobalt and red glazed plates. 12 5/8" and 14". $750+. 1,000. Courtesy of Jerry Kunz.

Glazed plates

The most high-style techniques were used to create these stunning and refined plates, some looking like tiles with a "Cuerda Seca" effect, with individual glaze colors applied in a wax-resist method after a pattern was "pounced" onto the plate. Some were first pressed into molded forms and then glazed. A wide variety of patterns and colors have been found in the ship, bird, and undersea garden plates.

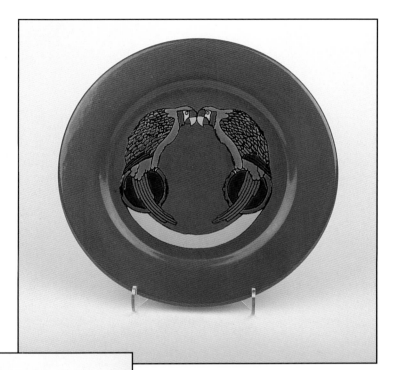

"Kissing Birds" plate. Red rim. Scarce design. 10". $1,000+. Courtesy of Jerry Kunz.

Undersea Garden plate. Blue rim. Popular and desirable design. 12 1/2". $1,000+. Courtesy of Mrs. Malcolm Renton.

"Shark" decorative plate. Cobalt rim. Scarce design. 10". $1,000+. Courtesy of Jerry Kunz.

Galleon plate. Found in all color combinations. A raised line design keeps the glazes from running together. 12". $650.

Undersea Garden plates. Mint green and Descanso Green rims. 10" & 13". Sizes did vary depending on clay and shrinkage. $1,000+. *Courtesy of Jerry Kunz.*

Raised design plates

Swordfish plates are found in single color glazes only in the one size. They were made throughout the entire period of pottery production, are found in all clay colors, and were molded pieces. The highest quality examples have very good definition from when the mold was new, so that the swordfish "reads well." A nice burn adds to the visual effect. Moorish plates are found in all color combinations including solid single glazes. The look is reminiscent of "Cuenca" tiles with solid raised lines that in effect keep the glazes from running together.

Undersea Garden plate with rare black rim. 13 3/4" and the largest size. NP. *Courtesy of Lillian Stone.*

Swordfish wall plate. Raised design. Monterey Brown. 14" diameter. $1,500+. *Courtesy of John Phelps.*

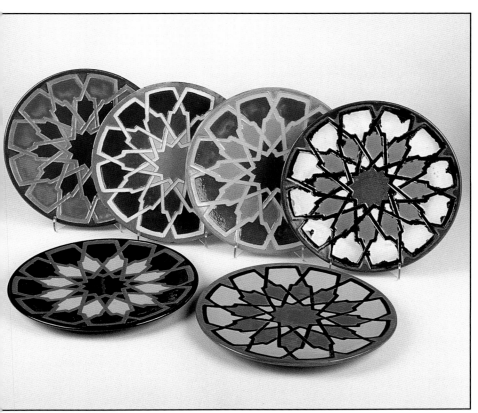

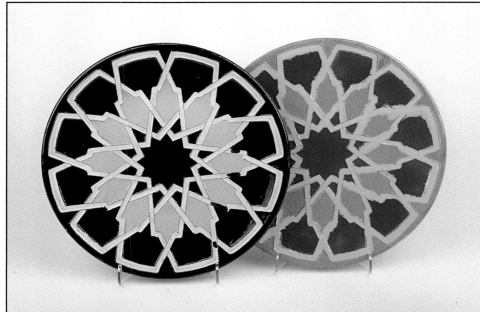

Two Moorish plates. Cuenca glaze technique. 11". $500+. *Courtesy of Carole Coates.*

Moorish plates in 6 different glaze combinations (also comes in single colors). Raised line design. 11" across. $500+. *Courtesy of Jerry Kunz.*

Moorish decorative plate. Stunning blue, red, and green glaze combination. 11 1/4". $500+. *Courtesy of Sandra Puttnam.*

Hand painted plates

Catalina's painted plates are highly prized and sought after. Up until this date little or no information had been discovered about the artists responsible. It is now known that there were three main female artists working in the employ of the pottery. They all painted scenes in enamel on solid color Catalina Island pottery plates and worked both indoors at the pottery plant and outdoors "plein air" on locations around Avalon. Island inspired themes were naturally very popular and scenes of ocean life, ships, Spanish Missions, and dancers predominate. Some were commissioned as trophies for special events and at least one portrays a real person working at the El Encanto open-air marketplace. Many of these "special event" plates are dated. Some plate backs have numbers which indicate subject matter. Whether or not a plate is signed does not affect its value. Prices vary based purely on aesthetics, although larger sizes usually command higher prices. Note the sizes of the plates in the captions. It is easy to lose perspective without anything to compare to. Many value the small painted salad size plates, which are rarely seen. Coasters are usually found with wildlife or birds, many most likely made and sold at the Bird Park.

Press releases of the day make mention of the fact that artists were at the pottery "painting and designing" wares. It is likely that these artists who did paintings on plates served the dual function as artists for the pictorial tile murals, as well as other decorative items. In an isolated community, which this was in the 1930s, many people served multiple functions. That these female artists, much like Bud Upton, will soon be credited with other "classic" pieces now seems a given.

Maude Chase (b. 1880, d. 1956)

Maude Elsie Hall Chase was a widow with four children when she came to Santa Ana from Nebraska in 1919. She had attended art school in Chicago where she met her husband Charles, who had earlier run a pottery in Ohio, and was a State Representative.

Catalina artist Maude Chase and her catch of the day. Notice the pearls and the proper dress! Dated Oct. 1931. *Courtesy of Carole Coates.*

She did "china painting," one of the only arts that was respectable for women at that time. Examples of her early work show an exceptional skill and an Art Nouveau influence. In Los Angeles she did interior design work for "movie people" in Beverly Hills that stemmed from her artist's studio where she decorated and sold hand painted lamp shades and house wares of her own design as well as "fired" items.

She arrived in Avalon in 1930 at 50 years of age accompanied by her youngest son, 19 year old Byron. Maude already had a reputation as a fine artist, so it makes sense that she had been hired first, and then a job was found for her son Byron at the pottery lab the following year. Her brother and a nephew worked at the pottery as well. (see Workers)

Many of the heirlooms Maude passed on to her family include black glazed items painted with gold decorations. It is assumed these represented her work, since the family only has painted items she personally made. Mrs. Chase was a Christian Science practitioner and was involved with the Society on the Island. Her eldest granddaughter Joan remembers going to Sunday services with her Grandma on Catalina, and how she was sought after as a singer who also accompanied herself on the piano. She was kind and loving but very outgoing. Her granddaughter Johnette describes Maude as having been "different from other people . . . she had an enthusiasm for everything and was always on the edge of her chair." When her signature is found, it reads "Chase." After her tenure with Catalina, she and her son Byron both helped out with the war effort by taking jobs at Douglas Aviation drawing design sketches for aircraft. After the war, she returned to painting with oils, but this time on canvas. She is a listed California artist.

"Bernard's Parakeets." Signed "Chase". 12 5/8". $950. *Courtesy of Lillian Stone.*

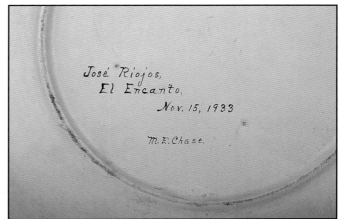

Detail from "The Candlemaker" plate.

Top: Scarlet Macaw with Palm. Signed "Chase". 12". $950. *Courtesy of Allan & Laurie Carter.*

Bottom: Killer whales in stylized ocean. Signed "Chase". 8". $750. *Courtesy of Allan & Laurie Carter.*

Top: "The Candlemaker." Signed "M. E. Chase" and titled "Jose Riojas. El Encanto. Nov 15. 1933". (Jose Riojas was the host of El Encanto). 12". NP. *Courtesy of Allan & Laurie Carter.*

Bottom: "San Juan Capistrano Mission." Signed "Chase". 13". $750. *Courtesy of Steven Hoefs.*

Desert Cactus scene on white plate. Signed "Chase". 12". $850. *Courtesy of Carole Coates.*

Schooner and Rowboat in Rough Seas. Signed "Chase". 13 1/2". $950+. Courtesy of Lillian Stone.

Top center: "Homeward Bound from Catalina." Signed "Chase". 13 1/2". $950+. Courtesy of Bob & Barbara Crow.

Bottom center: "Chase" signature, and numbers indicated scene.

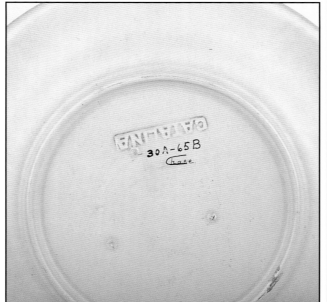

Florence M. Graham

We know little about Florence Graham's artistic background but we do know that she had flaming red hair and she was a very prolific painter. People from Avalon remember her as always running around town, probably because like Maude Chase she was kept busy painting plates on location around Avalon in the employ of the pottery. Young Roger Upton, Jr. remembers her fondly as "Mrs. Graham" and has some childhood pieces of Catalinaware with cartoon characters that were painted specifically for him by her. She had a daughter named "Eileen." Her signature on plates is usually accompanied by an artists easel ink stamp and reads either "G", "FMG", "F.M. Graham", or a vertical entwined "fm" which is another of her many marks.

"Santa Barbara Mission." Signed "F.M. Graham". 12". $750. Courtesy of Jerry Kunz.

Top: California Mission. Signed "F.M. Graham". 12 1/2". $750. *Courtesy of Sandra Puttnam.*

Bottom: "Carmel Mission Bell Tower." Signed "F.M. Graham". 13 1/2". $750. *Courtesy of Bob & Barbara Crow.*

Top: Spanish Mission with locals. Signed "F.M.G." 13". $750+. *Courtesy of Jerry Kunz.*

Bottom: Spanish Troubadour with Mandolin. Signed "F. M. Graham". 12". $950. *Courtesy of Allan & Laurie Carter.*

Top: Dancing Señorita. Signed "F.M. Graham". 12". $950+. *Courtesy of Sandra Puttnam.*

Bottom: "The Seranade" on horseback. Signed "F.M. Graham". 12". $950+. *Courtesy of Steven Hoefs.*

Top: The Vaquero. Dated "Aug. 10. 1935" signed with "fm" mark & artist palette. This plate and others like it are also called the "La Galendrina" plates because they lined the walls of the first Mexican restaurant in Olvera Street (which was owned by a friend of the Rentons). 10". $950. *Courtesy of Carole Coates.*

Bottom: Stagecoach scene. Signed "F. M. Graham". 14". $750. *Courtesy of Jerry Kunz.*

Top: "Catalina Chief Guate Mozen. El Encanto. Graham." A diminutive 8". $650. *Courtesy of Jerry Kunz.*

Bottom: Fighting cocks. Signed "G" for Graham. 14". $850. *Courtesy of Carole Coates.*

Top: "Character sketch of our President. Franklin D. Roosevelt." "F. M. Graham." Ink stamp with palette 12". $1,000+. *Courtesy of Jerry Kunz.*

Bottom: Seagulls in flight. Signed "Graham". 10". $850. *Courtesy of Allan & Laurie Carter.*

ailboat plate. Signed "Graham". 10". $850+. Courtesy
f Larry Harris.

"Ning Po" plate. Signed "F.M. Graham". 12". $1,000+.
Courtesy of Jerry Kunz.

"Historic Old Chinese Junk. Ning Po. At Catalina Ithmus"
signed F.M. Graham. $1,000+. Courtesy of Steven Hoefs.

"G" for Graham.

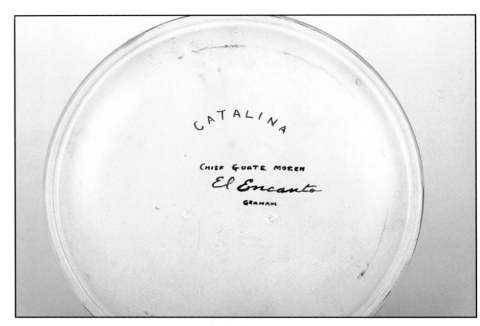

"Graham" signature.

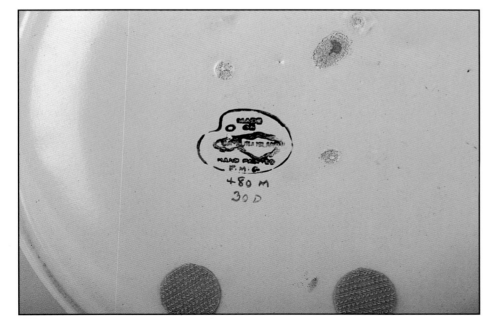

Artists palette logo in ink stamp, and "F.M.G.", Graham's initials.

Vertical entwined "fm".

Mrs. Strom

All that is currently known about this artist is that she was a woman, and she signed her work "Strom" or "Ström", which has been misidentified as Stroiti. It is hoped that more information will come forward from Islanders and/or family members for future editions.

Catalina Golf Trophy. Dated on front 1933. signed "Strom". 12". NP. Courtesy of Allan & Laurie Carter.

Boy on Burro. Signed "Strom". 13 3/4". $850. Courtesy of Bruce Gelker.

Left: "Ning Po". Signed "Strom". 13". $1,000. Courtesy of Allan & Laurie Carter.

Right: Spanish Galleon. Subtle pastel colors. Signed "Strom". 12 1/2". Courtesy of Bob & Barbara Crow.

"Strom signature".

Mr. Leslie Granteer, "S.J.W.", and unattributed works

Mr. Granteer was an occasional yet talented artist who is known for his painted Catalina plates as well as other graphic art work he did on the Island. He graduated Avalon High in 1932 and went to art school on the mainland, coming back for a short time before leaving again. This helps explain his sporadic and short-lived work for the pottery. He created the "Torqua" design still used on Catalina Island High's yearbook.

Sailing Vessel. Signed Granteer. 14". $1,000. Courtesy of Allan & Laurie Carter.

Ocean scene with seagull. Signed "Granteer". 14". $1,000. Courtesy of Ken DeHahn.

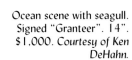

"Granteer" signature.

"S.J.W." signature.

Nesting Eagles. Signed "S.J.W." $750. *Courtesy of the Malcolm J. Renton Collection.*

Bald Eagle Head. Signed "SJW". 10". NP. *Courtesy of Lillian Stone.*

"Mr. Bim the Stork" a well-loved resident of the Bird Park. Initialed "SJW". Also signed "Wigley". 12". NP. *Courtesy of Ken DeHahn.*

Vaquero plate and Bronco Buster. Note size difference. 10" versus 7 7/8". $700. $500. *Courtesy of Carole Coates.*

California Quail. Unusual subject. "SJW". NP. *Courtesy of the Malcolm J. Renton Collection.*

Bronco Buster. 7 7/8" salad plate. No signature. $500. *Courtesy of Carole Coates.*

Cowboy on Horse. Unsigned. Possible attribution to Strom. 14". NP. Courtesy of Ken DeHahn.

Bucked Off. No attribution. 12 1/4". $750. Courtesy of Jerry Kunz.

Bucking Bronco. Unsigned. Possibly Strom. 14". $850. Courtesy of Ken DeHahn.

Spanish Galleon. Numbered but not signed. Possibly "Graham". 14". NP. Courtesy of Ken DeHahn.

Seagulls plate. No signature. 6" salad plate. $400+.
Courtesy of Steven Hoefs.

Moose coaster. Black paint on red glaze. No signature. $165.
Courtesy of Carole Coates.

Greek Goddess. White paint on blue glaze. Unusual subject. No
signature. 14". NP. *Courtesy of Ken DeHahn.*

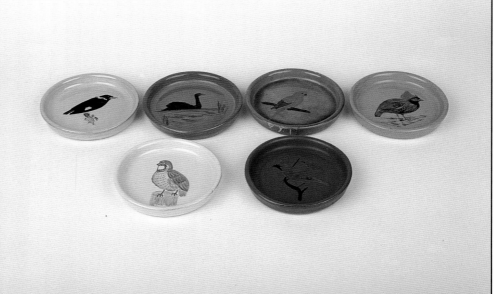

Left: Undersea Garden Scene
with Glass Bottom Boat at
Lover's Cove. Gold paint
technique. 6". NP. *Courtesy of
Steven Hoefs.*

Right: Coasters. Bird Park
residents and native animals.
Some artist signed. 4"
diameter. $100 - $200+.
*Courtesy of Allan & Laurie
Carter*

Roger "Bud" Upton, Sr. (b. 1900, d. 1986)

Artist and designer Bud Upton contributed to Island ware in many ways, not only on painted plates, but also to the original designs found in and on tile and novelties. Bud was well known for certain themes including eucalyptus trees, cowboys, western scenes, flowers, and birds. Based on this information, and specific stylistic details, an attribution to Upton might be in order on the glaze painted plates and many of the unsigned cowboy images. Bud Upton first came to Catalina in 1902 with his family on vacation but moved to Avalon for good in 1932. He was involved with designing for the pottery well before this time, since his most famous work was the Toucan Bird Mural designed c. 1930-31 during one of his summers on the Island (Upton interview 2000). This also gives us a date for the creation of the Bird murals, one a few years later than originally thought. This means that these murals must have been "retrofitted" to buildings built in earlier years. He arrived after a stint with Foster and Kleiser, the same advertising firm that Otis Shepard worked for in San Francisco. He worked with Shepard doing the Spanish lettering and scenic painting that's still found around town. Because of the Depression, people had to do more than one job to keep ahead and his son Roger remembers his dad as an all around painter, both of signs and buildings, although later of sought after oil paintings. Roger also recalls that his dad managed the El Encanto restaurant for the Renton's from 1934 to 1940, a choice job at the time. Keeping it all in the family, even Bud's brother Ed Upton ran the Catalina Pottery Shop on Casino Way for five years. Bud Upton is also famous for designing the "Siesta" ashtray. He was paid $1.50 for his original model, of which a plaster mold was made at the pottery. Over 60,000 of this combination ashtray-pipe holder-matchbook holders were produced and sold at the 1933 Chicago World's Fair for $2.50 each. He also designed the Treasure Chest cigarette box and the Goofyfoot Goat ashtray, as well as some impressive figural creations. His contributions to the art of the Island were certainly significant. Luckily, Mr. Upton lived long enough to both educate and inform us about this special time and to receive at least a small part of the recognition due him.

Roger "Bud" Upton painting at the under construction Casino in 1929. *Courtesy of Mr. and Mrs. Roger Upton.*

More palms. Glaze painted on yellow plate. 11".
$400. Courtesy of Carole Coates.

Toucan Bird Mural in
Avalon. One of the avian
residents of the Bird
Park named "Tooky" was
the Park's official symbol.
(Hillenger, Channel
Islands, 46)

Bucked Off Again. Slightly different view.
No signature. 12 1/4". $750. Courtesy of
Bruce Gelker.

Scarlet Macaw hand painted on bisque plate. Signed "RMU" on front for Roger Upton. 14". NP. *Courtesy of Ken DeHahn.*

Glaze painted plate. Unusual Eucalyptus trees black on green glaze. 12". $650. *Courtesy of Carole Coates.*

Glaze painted plate. Mission scene. Three glaze colors on yellow plate. 12". $450. *Courtesy of Carole Coates.*

Palm trees. Pastel glazes on white plate. 12 5/8". $400. *Courtesy of Allan & Laurie Carter.*

Palms Against the Water. Glaze painted on Toyon Red plate. 11". $400. *Courtesy of Allan & Laurie Carter.*

Glaze painted plate. Urns on green glaze. 11". $450. *Courtesy of Carole Coates.*

Color on the Table:
1929-1934

The effects of the Depression were being felt in full force in California and there were many times when only a half-crew was kept on at the pottery. Although the bird murals are shown in the 1934 catalog, tile was not produced in quantity, except for special orders and custom jobs. Luckily just as tile orders began to wane in 1931, Catalina's reputation for colorful dinnerware began to catch fire. This was in no small part due to the marketing ideas devised by D.M. Renton. He had a shop set up on Olvera Street as both a wholesale showroom and a retail store and marketed the dinnerware and art vases all across the country. Alma Overholt, publicist and writer, was hired to produce many effusive articles praising the pottery and its wares. From 1933 to 1936, the pottery was focused almost exclusively on the production of dinnerware. As opposed to pottery lines that were sold at Five and Dime stores, Catalina Island pottery was known as the "quality pottery." It was sold at the finest department stores around the country, including Bullock's, May's, Buffums, Marshall Fields, Lord and Taylors in New York, and Barker Brothers (an exclusive sales outlet for Monterey Furniture as well). Other than that, it could be bought on the Island or at a few high end spots such as the Los Angeles Biltmore, the Wrigley owned Arizona Biltmore, or at the Olvera Street Shop. Pottery was even sent to Mrs. Franklin Roosevelt from Olvera Street for use at one of her summer homes. (Wrigley-Renton correspondence). Many other notables and celebrities, then as now, were the proud owners of Catalinaware including Marion Davies, of William Randolph Hearst fame.

Tableware

There were many different lines of dinnerware produced by the pottery, some very early lines, some made throughout the life of the pottery, and others very short lived. Influences were as varied as the artware line and ranged from Arts and Crafts to Moorish to Deco. They include the rare Trojan line, the popular Rolled edge line, a Deco line, and the later and simple Plain line. All had service pieces, coffees, pitchers, and accessories made in a complimentary style. Quite a large quantity and variety of dinnerware was produced, and remarkably survives to this day, but the tremendous range of items makes for an embarrassment of riches. Not every teapot, plate, cup, bowl, casserole, or cream and sugar is shown here. A wide sampling of the most interesting items has been included. Many think that if it says "Catalina" it must automatically be rare. There are notable exceptions in service ware, but common din-

An attractive plain Console Set. Fruit or Flower Bowl (210). Candlestick Holder (380).

Refreshment Set (ing iced tea, lemo beverages. Six a Pitcher (104) 5-p (36) set of 6.

Interesting decorative pieces for every occasion. Fluted shallow Bowls (5 sizes), large 13½" (234), small, 6" (230). Vase (306) 10" high. Vase (305) 7½" high. Shell Ashtray (505).

This colorful Cereal Set will add mu cheer and brightness to the morni meal. Creamer (family style), (10 Sugar Bowl (51). Cereal or Fr Bowls (86).

nerware pieces generally do not command high prices. The good news is that it is possible for any collector to put together a nice set. Plates that are scratched or have glaze discoloration are less than desirable, because many Catalina aficionados use their dinnerware for special occasions, sans steak knives and dishwashers, of course. It's also a good idea not to store acidic foods overnight because of potential lead leaching, but there's otherwise little need for concern. Catalina's Toyon Red glaze was said to have used uranium, perhaps accounting for it's 10% additional price, but while

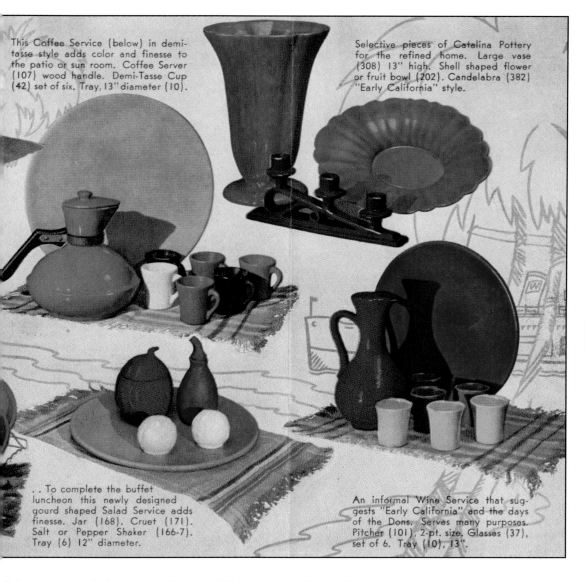

This Coffee Service (below) in demi-tasse style adds color and finesse to the patio or sun room. Coffee Server (107) wood handle. Demi-Tasse Cup (42) set of six. Tray, 13" diameter (10).

Selective pieces of Catalina Pottery for the refined home. Large vase (308) 13" high. Shell shaped flower or fruit bowl (202). Candelabra (382) "Early California" style.

. . To complete the buffet luncheon this newly designed gourd shaped Salad Service adds finesse. Jar (168). Cruet (171). Salt or Pepper Shaker (166-7). Tray (6) 12" diameter.

An informal Wine Service that suggests "Early California" and the days of the Dons. Serves many purposes. Pitcher (101), 2-pt. size. Glasses (37), set of 6. Tray (10), 13".

Geiger counters light up over Fiesta and Bauer orange, Toyon Red doesn't even move the needle.

Service plates could be scalloped or plain and used for decoration or appetizers. Seashell shapes were used for serving pieces as well as flower bowls. Some were embellished with iron ivy tendrils or copper holders. Candy dishes had a stylish edge. Salt and pepper shakers shaped like Señors and Señoritas or Cacti gave it a pleasant touch of whimsy. Any mix and match of colors would do for bowls, plates, pitchers, and teapots.

Rolled edge plates. From 6" up to 18". $15 - $250. *Courtesy of Carole Coates.*

Plain line plates. Six graduated sizes. 12", 11", 10", 9", 8", and 7". Various colors & prices. Tend to be the most affordable plates, except in large sizes or scarce glazes. *Courtesy of Jerry Kunz.*

Dinnerware place settings with rolled edge & grill plates. *Courtesy of Carole Coates.*

Largest charger to luncheon plate. Turquoise and yellow. 18" and 8". $250 and $35. *Courtesy of Carole Coates.*

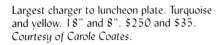

Small salad and desert plates. See if you can pick out five different lines. All glazes. 7" to 6". $10 to $30 each. *Courtesy of Jerry Kunz.*

Cereal, soup, and small dinnerware bowls, ranging from 6" to 3". $15 - $65. *Courtesy of Jerry Kunz.*

Dinnerware place settings.

Promotional pitcher. Highly unusual form. High gloss green glaze. Inscribed "The May Co. 6-21-32 C. Hansen". The bottom is inscribed "W.H. Brown". 11" high. NP. *Courtesy of Bob & Barbara Crow.*

Grill plate. Blue glaze. These plates are hard to find undamaged. $85+. *Courtesy of Carole Coates.*

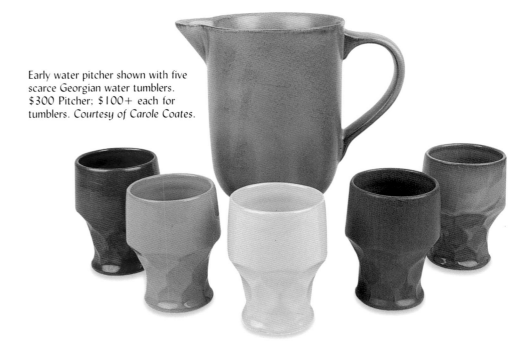

Early water pitcher shown with five scarce Georgian water tumblers. $300 Pitcher; $100+ each for tumblers. *Courtesy of Carole Coates.*

Large handled pitcher. Blue. 7" high to lip. $300+. *Courtesy of Carole Coates.*

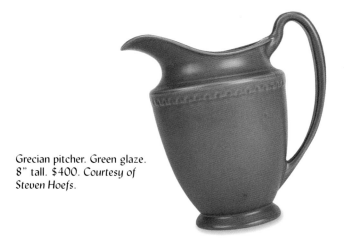

Grecian pitcher. Green glaze. 8" tall. $400. *Courtesy of Steven Hoefs.*

Large water pitcher. Blends two known forms. Green glaze. For once a truly handscratched "Catalina". 9" tall. *Courtesy of Bob & Barbara Crow.*

Beverage set. Handled pitcher & wine cups on charger (from the estate of Marion Davies, girlfriend of William Randolph Hearst). 9" high pitcher. 2" high cups. NP. *Courtesy of Carole Coates.*

Scalloped edge service plates with wine pitcher. Turquoise and green. Plates 11" and 7" across. $85 and $55. 9" pitcher: $200. *Courtesy of Carole Coates.*

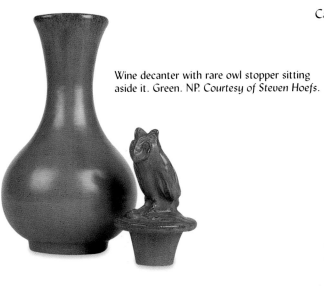

Wine decanter with rare owl stopper sitting aside it. Green. NP. *Courtesy of Steven Hoefs.*

Wine decanter with rare owl stopper. 13" tall. *Courtesy of Steven Hoefs.*

An assortment of pitchers and cups to show scale. *Courtesy of Carole Coates.*

Wine carafe with rare Penguin figurine stopper. Catalina Blue. 12 1/2" tall. NP. *Courtesy of Allan & Laurie Carter.*

Hexagonal water bottle. Rarer form. Red glaze. 7" tall. $350+. *Courtesy of Carole Coates.*

Beverage set. Water pitcher with cups in original iron holder. 16" high. Backed by an 18" Toyon Red charger. NP. *Courtesy o[f] Allan & Laurie Carter.*

Deco coffee pot with demitasse cups. Very hard to find with lid. Wooden handle. Green. Pot: $350 with lid, $95 without. Cups: $20+ each. 10 1/2" high and 2" high. *Courtesy of Carole Coates.*

Wooden handled coffee carafes. Turquoise, white, and red. 8" high. $150+ with lid. $50 without. *Courtesy of Carole Coates.*

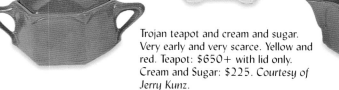

Trojan teapot and cream and sugar. Very early and very scarce. Yellow and red. Teapot: $650+ with lid only. Cream and Sugar: $225. *Courtesy of Jerry Kunz.*

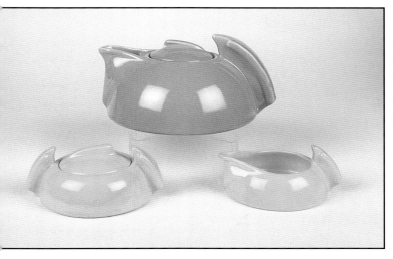

Deco teapot and matching cream and sugar. Early and rare form. 4" and 2" tall. Pot: $650+. Cream and Sugar: $225. *Courtesy of Jerry Kunz.*

Individual creamer. Yellow. 1" high. Hard to find. Unmarked with many look-alikes. $55. *Courtesy of Carole Coates.*

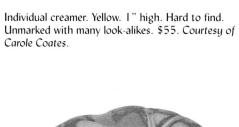

Salt cellar. Raised design. Seafoam. 2" across. $45. *Courtesy of Carole Coates.*

eamers and sugars. en and seafoam. 2 1/8" and 2" tall. $150 each pair. *Courtesy of Jerry Kunz.*

Shrimp icer set. Three legged and three parts: bottom, ring, and glass insert. Red and turquoise. 3" high. $225. Bottom only: $75. *Courtesy of Carole Coates.*

Deco creamers and sugars. Raised design. 2" high red and green glazed pairs. $300 each pair. *Courtesy of Jerry Kunz.*

Individual casseroles. Rarely found with lids. Red, yellow, and white. 3" high. $125 each. *Courtesy of Carole Coates.*

Condiment set. Mixed colors.

Refrigerator jar with lid. This is early "tupperware," not to be confused with the similar looking custards. Smallest of four sizes at 2" tall. $45 with lid only. *Courtesy of Carole Coates.*

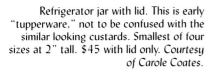

Custard cup set in original box. 2" high. NP. Individual custards: $25 each. *Courtesy of Carole Coates.*

Condiment set on tray. Mayonnaise jar: $150 with lid; vinegar gourd cruet: $135 with lid; gourd salt and pepper: $135; pickle toothpick holder: $125; tray: $225. *Courtesy of Carole Coates.*

Celery dish. Very hard to find form. Seafoam. 7 1/4". $145. *Courtesy of Bob & Barbara Crow.*

Handled cloverleaf candy dish. Yellow glaze. This piece is found more commonly without a handle. 9" across. $250+. *Courtesy of Jerry Kunz.*

Serving plate with original raffia coated copper handle. Seafoam glaze. $200+. *Courtesy of Carole Coates.*

Serving platter in original island iron holder with ivy details. Monterey Brown. 14 1/4" Plate: $250; holder: $225. *Courtesy of Lillian Stone and Sandra Puttnam.*

Tortilla warmer with raised design lid. Monterey Brown glaze. The very rarest of the dinnerware pieces, with great definition and in a scarce glaze. 10" diameter, 3" high. $1,500+ only with a lid and in mint condition. *Courtesy of John Phelps.*

Raised design beer stein. Hardly ever seen. 5" tall. $250. *Courtesy of Allan & Laurie Carter.*

Assortment of handled mugs. All in Monterey Brown glaze. Ranging from 6" to 2". $40 - $500. In normal glazes the price range would be $25 - $250. *Courtesy of John Phelps.*

Deco chocolate mugs. Two different raised designs. Hard to find. 4" tall. $100+.

Coffee cups and saucers. Straight sided. 5" diameter saucer. 2 1/8" high cup. $55+ each. *Courtesy of Carole Coates.*

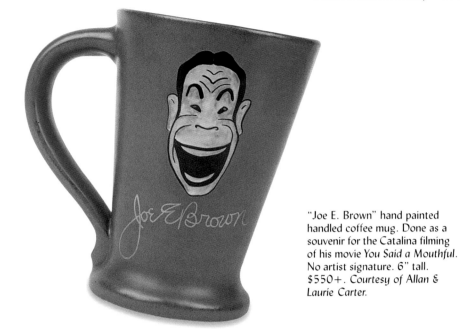

"Joe E. Brown" hand painted handled coffee mug. Done as a souvenir for the Catalina filming of his movie *You Said a Mouthful.* No artist signature. 6" tall. $550+. *Courtesy of Allan & Laurie Carter.*

Coffee cups and mugs. See if you can spot the various differences. *Courtesy of Jerry Kunz.*

Five mixing bowls. Nesting ring on top outside. Various colors and sizes. $95 - $350.

Punch bowl & cups. 14" across, 5" high. 2" high cups. $600 bowl. $60 each cup. *Courtesy of Carole Coates.*

Chips and Dips. Serving charger with indented center & bowl. Red and green. 18" and 8" diameters. $500 set. *Courtesy of Carole Coates.*

Another view of punch bowl.

Cactus salt and pepper shakers. Size varies quite charmingly. 3" high. $225+ pair. *Courtesy of Carole Coates.*

Señor and Señorita salt and pepper shakers. 4" high. $225 pair in common glazes.

Gourd salt and peppers. Catalina (front pair) vs. Japanese look-alike (back pair). 2 3/8" high vs 2" high. Seafoam & red. $125 Catalina pair, $15 pair others. *Courtesy of Jerry Kunz.*

Señor & Señorita salt & pepper shakers. 4" high. Blue and red. Wonderful when found with any original cold paint on serape & dress. $225+ pair *Courtesy of Carole Coates.*

Raised design salt and pepper in original copper holder. Blue. 2" tall. $150+ set. *Courtesy of Carole Coates.*

Tulip salt and pepper shakers. Beware of Japanese look-alikes. Green and black glaze. $125 pair and NP. *Courtesy of Carole Coates.*

Candlesticks and Centerpieces

Candlesticks and candelabras were among the many inventive and unique Catalina creations. Equally at home on the table, mantle, or entry as an accent wherever a splash of drama and romance was needed in the home. Figural flower frogs in the shape of cranes or pelicans perched on top of centerpiece bowls, and most other bowls could double for chips or fruit display.

Cactus candleholders. Raised "stickers" detail. Hard to find. Green. 6 3/8" tall. $800+ each. *Courtesy of Bill Noonan and Carole Coates.*

Entry table with display of Catalina Blue, including candlesticks. *Courtesy of Allan and Laurie Carter.*

Eight candleholders in various forms and colors for size perspective.

Candlesticks. Two pairs. Yellow and blue. 3" & 5". $195 and $250 pair. Courtesy of Jerry Kunz.

Signature on 3" candlesticks.

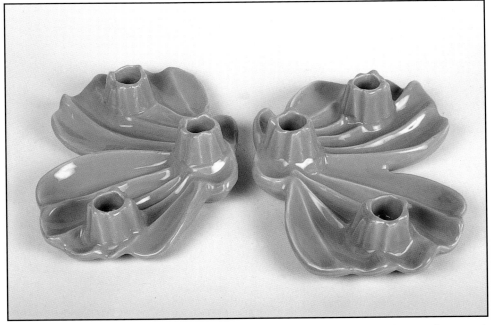

Candleholders. Blue. Raised detail on base. 5" high. $295. Courtesy of Carole Coates.

Pair of shell candelabras. Holds six candles altogether. Turquoise. 10" across. $500+ pair. Courtesy of Carole Coates.

Handled candleholder. 4 3/4" across base. Can be used singly or in pairs. $195 single. *Courtesy of Carole Coates.*

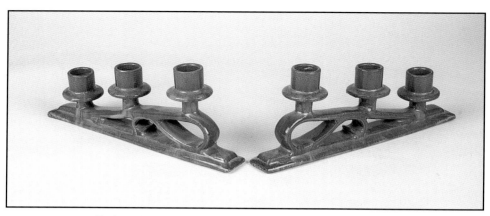

Triple candelabras. Seafoam. $1,000+ pair. *Courtesy of Jerry Kunz.*

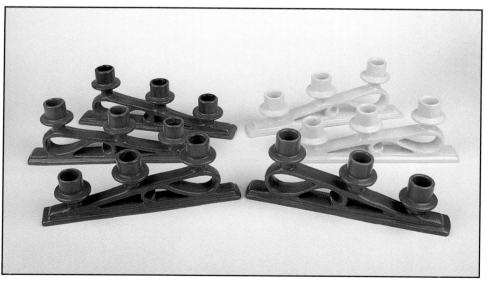

Triple candelabras. Only a pair has the right look. Blue, green and white. 12" base. 5" at highest point. $650+ pair. *Courtesy of Carole Coates.*

Catalina charger and bowl in metal stand. 12" and 9". NP. *Courtesy of Carole Coates.*

Bowl in metal holder. Notice the metal was formed in the shape of a Catalina vase! Blue glaze. 8" diameter bowl. NP. *Courtesy of Carole Coates.*

Fluted bowl set. Monterey Brown. They do "nest." 11", 9", and 7". $500+ set. *Courtesy of John Phelps*

Scalloped bowls. Two versions. One with pedestal foot. Red glaze. 6" and 8" across. $350 footed, $125 without. *Courtesy of Jerry Kunz.*

Conical centerpiece bowls. Turquoise and green. 16" and 12" across. $500+, $300. *Courtesy of Carole Coates.*

Deco raised design flare bowl. Tough to find. Green glaze. 12" across. $400. *Courtesy of Jerry Kunz.*

Footed compote. Yellow glaze. 9" across, 5" high. $225. *Courtesy of Jerry Kunz.*

Hexagonal bowl. Sits on three "feet." Early form. Turquoise on red clay. 11" across. $250+. *Courtesy of Jerry Kunz.*

Shell serving dish. Red glaze. Largest of two sizes. 14". $195. *Courtesy of Jerry Kunz.*

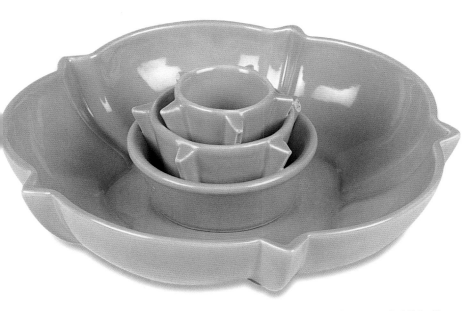

Starlight design centerpiece bowl with spiky flower frog. Turquoise glaze. 13" across. 5 1/3" tall. $195. Courtesy of Jerry Kunz.

Fluted centerpiece bowl in largest size. Scarce seafoam glaze with Crane flower frog. 17" across. 7 1/8" high to top of crane. $800+ in this glaze. Courtesy of Jerry Kunz.

Smallest fluted centerpiece bowl with teeny flower frog. 8" across. Blue. $195 with frog. Courtesy of Carole Coates.

Flower frogs. White Pelican with hand painted details. Blue Crane. 3-tiered plain frog is 7" across and smallest frog is only 1 3/8" across. Courtesy of Allan & Laurie Carter.

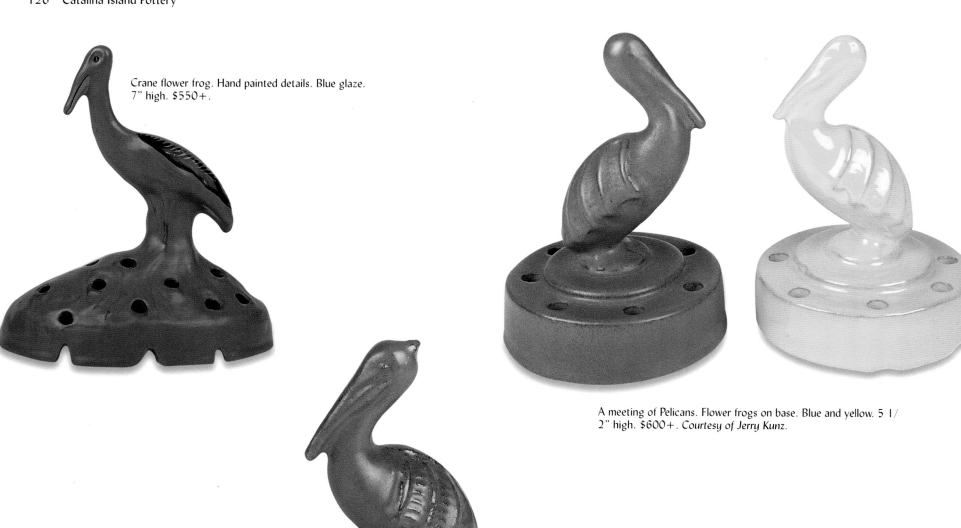

Crane flower frog. Hand painted details. Blue glaze. 7" high. $550+.

A meeting of Pelicans. Flower frogs on base. Blue and yellow. 5 1/2" high. $600+. *Courtesy of Jerry Kunz.*

Blue Pelican frog. Shallow base. 5" high. $600+. *Courtesy of Steven Hoefs.*

Large four-legged flower frog. Monterey Brown. 8".
$150. *Courtesy of John Phelps.*

Two Crane flower frogs and tiered plain versions. For size comparison.

Catalina Tile Treasures

Tile accents. Atwater Hotel Entrance, Avalon. Blue with yellow arrows, black trim.

In the late 1920s and early 1930s, tile was king. The California tile industry was booming and a multitude of companies sprang up to service the demand. Ceramic engineers were mainly trained at Washington State, the University of Illinois, and Ohio State to fill the burgeoning industry. Students were brought to Southern California for summer jobs and "scouted" by Gladding McBean, then the largest large tile and pottery maker in the United States. Gladding McBean had already gained a reputation as a "graduate school" to many in the ceramics field and would soon come to dominate the field by taking over many concerns. Considered one of the more stable employers in the ceramics industry, a job with them was the pinnacle of many careers and with that comes another Catalina connection.

John Wilde started as the "Tile Factory" plant supervisor by at least 1931 and remained until 1936, when he was noted as being the supervisor of the pottery plant. (Windle 1931) He was "loaned" from Ponoma Tile Company where he worked with his father, Fred Wilde. Fred was an English ceramist with a brilliant reputation for both quality tile work and rich glaze formulations, in other words a "tile man." Fred Wilde was mentioned earlier as being responsible for creating the decorative tiles that made such a sensation at the Panama Pacific Exhibition. He specialized in Spanish style tiles during his tenure at Northern California's renowned Arequipa Pottery from 1916 to 1918, and young John was with him there. The movement of artists, chemists, and glazes from one company to another, and how their techniques evolved through the years as new styles and trends emerged, is a fascinating although often frustrating study. As the baton was passed from the Arts and Crafts movement to the Spanish Revival, the common roots they shared are apparent.

John Wilde either brought with him his father's gift for color, his secret glaze formulas, or both, and it is unclear whether an attribution to Mr. Haldeman or Mr. Wilde, or another mystery ceramist, is in order for many colors and designs from this period. Around this time is when the "Monterey Brown" and "Seafoam" glazes were developed, rich sophisticated glazes that were possibly of Haldeman's, John's, or Fred Wilde's invention. John rejoined his father at Ponoma Tile at the end of his Catalina tenure in 1936, and later continued his career at Gladding McBean. Obsidian Black with gold painting was a style that emerged during his tenure as well. A tile given to Mr. Renton and dated 1931 exists as a test and gives us a date for the beginning of this technique's use.

Architectural use of Catalina Island tiles on the Wrigley Memorial, Avalon, California.

Tiled Avalon storefront. Currently the Catalina Crafters shop. Incorporates five historic Bird Murals. It is believed that the panel below the window is a vintage mainland replacement.

Black field tile with gold paint reading "D.M. Renton. Esq. Catalina. 1931". Possibly a test piece for the gold paint under glaze technique. NP. *Courtesy of the Malcolm J. Renton Collection.*

This patio tile fountain installation incorporated "wavy" border tiles and elsewhere used the earliest high quality tiles made (c. 1930). *Courtesy of Dr. Staff.*

Card suites four tile set. Used in the corner of gaming tables. Low fire gold paint. Unset 5 7/8". NP. *Courtesy of Allan & Laurie Carter.*

Pictorial Murals

Leaping Marlins, Casinos, airplanes, and birds were some of the many subjects covered by the famous glazed Catalina tile murals. The Bird Murals are found extensively around the Island. But which came first, the birds or the bird tiles? Recent evidence suggests that the initial 1928 construction at the Bird Park (which in its heyday housed a collection of over 3,000 rare and exotic birds and was open free to the public) *did not* include any Bird Murals. It is likely that instead the real birds were the inspiration and the tiles were retrofitted in a later improvement of 1930.

The Patio at Casa Solana, D.M. Renton's former home, contains the only known single Casino tile. *Courtesy of the Malcolm J. Renton Collection.*

31. This gives us a later and more likely date for the Bird Murals' creation, and is a similar treatment to the known tile retrofitting of the Chimes Tower and other downtown buildings in the 1930s.

Designed for stucco walls, tables, or to be hung from Island made iron frames, these pictorial tiles are comprised of one, two, four, and even fifteen tile sets to make a scene. The glazed tiles are usually done in a wax resist method, although some use a raised line technique for glaze separation.

Very unusual hand painted Leaping Swordfish tile. NP. *Courtesy of Larry Harris.*

Marlin four tile set with borders in cast iron base (not shown). 12" x 12". $3,000. *Courtesy of Jerry Kunz.*

Toucan Bird Mural set. Six 5 5/8" tiles make the scene. Overall size ungrouted: 17 5/8" x 11". $2,000+. *Courtesy of Carole Coates.*

Green Macaw Bird Mural set. Six 5 5/8" tiles make the scene. Unset tiles: $2,000+. *Courtesy of Carole Coates.*

Double Scarlet Macaw Bird Mural set. Six 5 5/8" tiles make the scene. $2,000+. *Courtesy of Carole Coates.*

Lorikeet Bird Mural set. Six 5 5/8" tiles make the scene. $2,000+. *Courtesy of Carole Coates.*

Crested Crane mural in vintage non-Island iron frame. Six 5 5/8" tiles make the scene. One of the harder to find bird scenes. Note: Single tiles from this or any bird set do not command high prices. $2,800. *Courtesy of Carole Coates.*

Green Macaw Bird Mural in original Island iron hanger with border tiles in black and green. Marked in ink stamp on back "Catalina Clay Products". $2,800+. *Courtesy of Carole Coates.*

"Catalina Clay Products" ink stamp on back of Green Macaw Bird Mural.

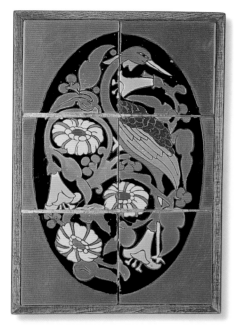

"Fantasy" or Magic Bird Mural. 18" tall x 11" across. No border tiles. Contemporary wood frame. Another hard to find mural. $2,500+. *Courtesy of Jerry Kunz.*

Marlin four tile set. Has dark blue top fin detail on fish. Seen done with green top fin as well. In cast iron base (not shown). No border tiles. 12" x 12". $3,000+. *Courtesy of John Phelps.*

"Fantasy" Bird Mural in original iron holder. Orange and black border tiles. $2,800+. *Courtesy of Allan & Laurie Carter.*

Rarely seen Seagull tile. One of a two tile set. NP. *Courtesy of Larry Harris.*

"Mystery" tile on stucco. This Catalina tile is found on two sites on the Island and belongs to an undersea scene that no one has ever seen.

Postcard of the Hamilton Cove Amphibian Airport. The circular "lazy susan" for turning planes around was thought up by Phillip Wrigley. It was said to be the smallest airport in the world with the longest runway . . . the Pacific Ocean. *Courtesy of John Phelps.*

In the "Catalina" world very exciting discoveries are constantly being made, and quite recently some hand painted Western wall murals were discovered that had not even been known to exist.

"Catalina Roundup." Hand painted mural on white field tiles in original iron frame. Other than hand painted table scenes, these wall murals are the first of their kind to surface. NP. *Courtesy of JimPhillips and Gerald Orcholski.*

"Catalina Bronco." Hand painted mural in original iron frame. Six 6" tiles make the scene. NP. *Courtesy of JimPhillips and Gerald Orcholski.*

Tile "hugger" Bill Noonan standing next to the cupola from the Hamilton Cove airport that was saved and reinstalled in situ. Some reproduction tiles were used for repair. The airport was torn down in 1966.

"W" tile saved from a wall at the Hamilton Cove Airport. One of only three or four known to exist. "W" stands for Wilmington Transportation, not Wrigley. 11 5/8" wide x 11" tall. NP. *Courtesy of John Phelps.*

The most unique of all the glazed tiles are those associated with aviation, a special love of Phillip Wrigley, who was an early supporter and innovator of aviation and its many uses for the Island.

Detail of Hamilton Cove Cupola.

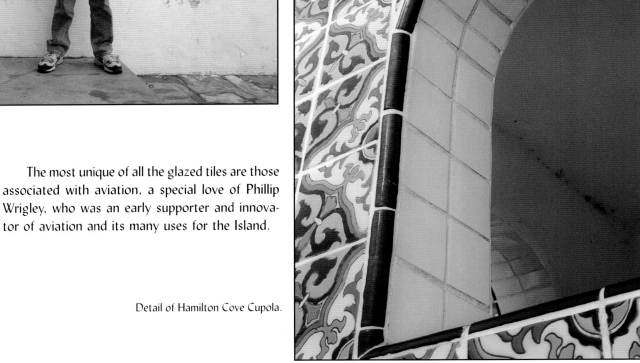

Airplane tile. Raised "Catalina" on wings. "W" lightly raised on blue glazed background. Dark red clay. 3". $350. *Courtesy of Carole Coates.*

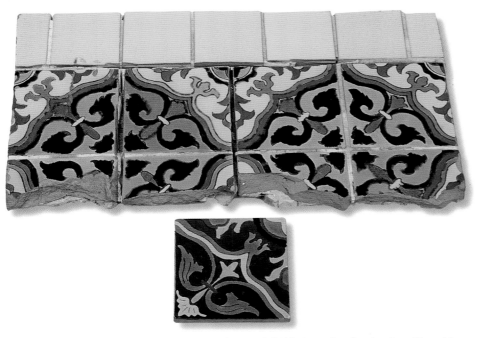

Tile fragment from Hamilton Cove Amphibian Airport. 5 7/8" tiles with yellow borders. Alongside it is a similar looking tile believed to be from another California maker.

Catalina Seaplane mural in contemporary iron wall plaque. This was rescued from the Hamilton Cove Airport where the Wilmington-Catalina Airlines was formed by P.K. Wrigley in 1931. NP. *Courtesy of the Catalina Island Museum.*

Seaplane tile mural entitled "Douglas Dolphin." 29" long x 17" tall. Comprised of fifteen 5 7/8" tiles. One of only three or four known to exist. NP. *Courtesy of Allan & Laurie Carter.*

Decorative Tile

Spanish, Moorish, and floral themes predominate on decorative tiles designed to be used in homes and patios or on tables. It was common for ancient tile designs from Turkey and Spain to be used as inspiration. Some are sets of four, six, or nine tiles and others are stand-alone "tea tiles" that could be used as trivets or for lamps. In 1930, the tile fronted Bank Building (now C.C. Gallagher) was built on Crescent Avenue utilizing the rarely seen single Marlin tiles, and early Lion head "bookends" as "toppers" on tile columns. A private fountain on the Island that also dates from 1930 uses the Marlin and early star tiles, providing us with additional dating information. In 1931, Catalina decorative tile was used extensively for the pool and clubhouse that were added to the Wrigley's newly acquired Arizona Biltmore Hotel as well as for the building of their neighboring Arizona residence. On Catalina in the early 1930s, special tile was used in the building of the beautiful Hamilton Cove Airport (removed in 1965) and for Phillip Wrigley's Rancho Escondido, his world class Arabian Horse Ranch located in the Island's interior.

Spectacular tile fronted former bank building now home to the C.C. Gallagher shop. Contains the rarely seen single Marlin tiles as well as a very detailed floral panel over the doorway. Two niches with iron work. Red clay lion tile/bookends stand guard over all.

Scarce floral tile set. Nine tiles make the set, including "pie" shaped ends. Black border incorporated onto tiles. 18" diameter. Glazed in orange, black, and teal on yellow background. $2,000+. *Courtesy of Carole Coates*

Floral panel over doorway on Crescent Avenue. The border tiles have sea creatures leaping about, and is done in a very high quality technique reminiscent of Malibu Tiles.

Urn design four tile set. Blue, red, and green accents on a pale yellow background. Incorporated border design. 5 7/8" tiles. $1,200 set. *Courtesy of Allan & Laurie Carter.*

Side detail of floral set. Many high quality tile sets show glaze drips off the sides.

Star four tile set. Very high gloss finish. 5" tiles. $1,000. *Courtesy of Allan & Laurie Carter.*

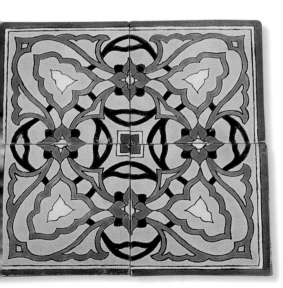

Octagonal four tile set. Black with yellow scroll pattern. 16" diameter. $850. *Courtesy of Carole Coates.*

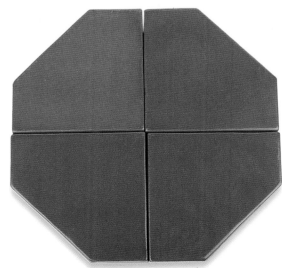

Floral four tile set. Cobalt, light blue, white, and black glazes on a light green background. Border incorporated onto tiles. Very high gloss finish. $1,200 set.

Octagonal four tile set. Red glaze solid tiles. This example is signed, but not all were. Used for walls or tables. 12" across. Unset. $400. *Courtesy of Carole Coates.*

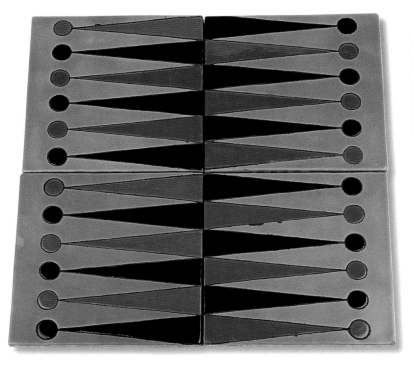

Backgammon tile set. Four 8" tiles. Unset. Orange & black on tan background. Don't try playing backgammon with the tiles facing this way! $950+ set, depending on color combination. *Courtesy of Carole Coates.*

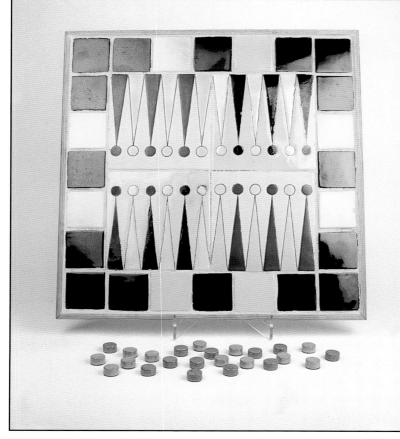

Backgammon four tile set. Green, yellow, and black glazes. With border tiles set in contemporary wood frame. NP. *Courtesy of Mrs. Malcolm Renton.*

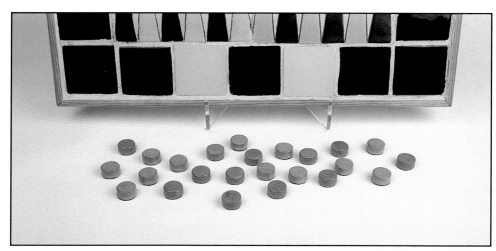

Original pottery playing pieces in green and red glazes. 1" diameter. Although documented in press releases in th 1930s, this is the first time a full set has been photographed. NP. *Courtesy of Mrs. Malcolm Renton.*

"This Way to Talking Mynahs" Bird Park "Directional" Tile. Extremely rare hand painted on white glazed field tile. 5 15/16". NP. *Courtesy of Sandra Puttnam.*

Postcard printed by Western Publishing & Novelty Company, Los Angeles, depicts the Bird Park.

Pinwheel tile. Done in blue, red, yellow, and white. 5 5/8". $200+. Courtesy of Carole Coates.

Stucco wall in Avalon with assorted tile "seconds" used as accents. Added in the "Old California" styling starting in 1934.

"Parrot Finch –Australia" Bird Park ID tile. 5 5/8". NP. Courtesy of Catalina Island Museum.

Assortment of patterned tiles. 5 5/8". $225 - $300+. *Courtesy of Carole Coates.*

Tile comparison. Catalina on the right is similar to Hamilton Cove tiles and others found around Avalon. Left is a similar copy by an unknown vintage maker. *Courtesy of Carole Coates.*

Pinwheel tiles. 5 5/8". Done in four different glaze combinations. $250+. *Courtesy of Larry Harris.*

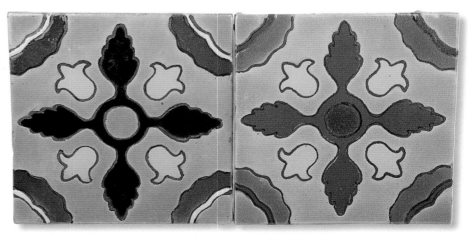

Two Leaf and Flower tiles. Different glaze combinations. 5 5/8". $225. *Courtesy of Carole Coates.*

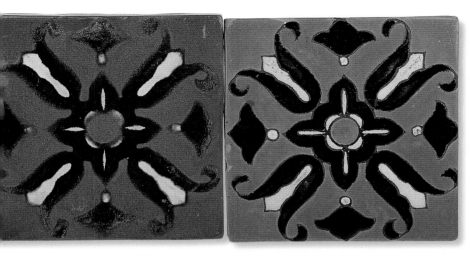

loral pattern tiles. Note the difference in execution. One is very blurry, one quite distinct. 5 5/8".
150 - 250. *Courtesy of Carole Coates.*

Assortment of tea tiles and decorative tiles. 5 5/8". $150 - $250. *Courtesy of Carole Coates.*

ive assorted star tiles. Different glaze combinations. These are among the earliest high-quality glazed
iles produced, c. 1930. *Courtesy of Carole Coates.*

Tile backs of those same six tiles in order. Notice the wide variety of different clay colors. This was true for pottery as well, but isn't as easy to see.

Tiled bench from the Wrigley Memorial.

Round Dragon tile from smoking stand. Glazed sides indicate tile that can "stand alone." Green and yellow on orange background. Very hard to find. 9" diameter. $850+. *Courtesy of Carole Coates.*

Another example of the Dragon tile with a unglazed example in the same size.

The same "Wrigley Memorial" tiles. Blue and green on tan background. Four 5 7/8" tiles. Unset. $750 set. *Courtesy of Carole Coates.*

Close up of original ink stamp on back of tea tile felt.

The three patterns of the "Stand Alone" Tea Tiles. Aztec, "Kissing Fish," and Deco Flowers in raised designs. Exceptional examples in both glaze and form. Monterey Brown. Light red clay. 6". $600+ each. *Courtesy of Bill Noonan.*

Tea tiles. Kissing Fish, Aztec, and Deco Flowers from left to right. Note the crisp delineation on the Fish tile, and compare clay colors. Green glaze. All signed. $350+ each. *Courtesy of Carole Coates.*

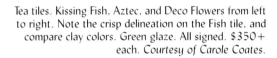

Tile backs of the three green tea tiles.

Tables and Furniture

Iron and Wood Bases, Smoke Stands

Catalina had a foundry and a furniture shop that made iron accessories, table bases, plant holders, and smoke stands. Glazed tile gaming sets for backgammon and checkers, side tables, patio tables, and more were all in demand. Rarely seen desert and wagon scenes were hand painted and incorporated onto tile tables. In 1932, tile tables were the "sensation" of the San Francisco Furniture Show. Los Angeles distributor C.R. Kayser advertised Catalina tables as having that "Alta California influence" and promoted the tile patterns as being "authentic reproductions of English, Italian, and Spanish period motifs." (Kayser Ad 1932) Other mainland firms installed the tiles in table bases as well, and the ultimate piece of Catalina tile furniture finds its expression in Monterey Furniture's Prohibition Bar.

Commemorative Rotary tile. Gold low fire paint on blue glazed tile. Many Islanders are and were Rotarians. Dated "May 6 - 7 - 8 - 1931." 3" x 3". $150. *Courtesy of Allan & Laurie Carter.*

An assortment of field tile and border tiles in different sizes and colors.

Catalina Tables

Catalina Tables

End table with center decorated tile. Brown and green borders. 17" high original Island wooden base. Tile dimensions: 12" square. This is one of the more commonly seen Catalina tables. $450. Courtesy of Carole Coates.

Side table with six red tiles. Usually found in a more common four tile version. Original Island wooden base. 17" high. 12" x 18" tile overall. $750. Courtesy of Carole Coates

Tall lamp table set with center tile. Seven tiles make the set. Green. Original Island wood base. At 25" high, it is a scarce size. Also found in a 17" version. $950. Courtesy of Carole Coates.

Round end table. Original Island wooden base. Four legged. Desirable nine tile set in green glaze. 18" tall. 18" tile diameter. Also found in a taller lamp table version. $1,000+. Courtesy of Bill Noonan.

Single, circular tile table. Original Island wooden base. Three legged. 9 5/8" tile in a black glaze. Hard to find. $850. Courtesy of Allan & Laurie Carter.

Floral tile table. Orange, green, and yellow on a black background. Original Island base. Four legs. Four tiles. 17" high. 12" diameter tiles only. 26" tall. $650. *Courtesy of Carole Coates.*

Tile side table. Black solid tiles mix with floral pattern tiles. White, yellow, blue, and green with a red background. Seven tiles make the set. 12" tile diameter. Wooden. 17" high. Six legs. $650. *Courtesy of Carole Coates.*

Moorish design tile table. Extremely colorful and detailed tile pattern. Not often seen. 16" tile diameter. 26" tall table. NP. *Courtesy of Carole Coates.*

Closeup showing tile detail.

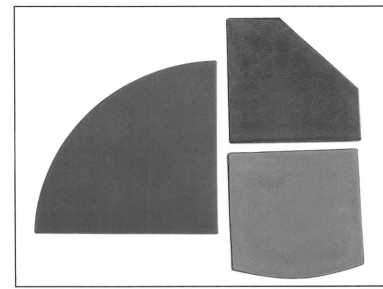

Moorish tile entry table. This same pattern is installed over the entrance to the old Bank Building on Crescent Avenue in Avalon. Highly detailed "Sea Creature" borders. Table in wooden base. Tiles are 15" square including borders. N.P. *Courtesy of Allan and Laurie Carter.*

Detail of tile table pieces.

Single geometric tile table. 5 7/8" tile set in wood, on early cast iron base. This base was made on the Mainland before the Island iron shop geared up, but was assembled on the Island. It is found with other tops. $500. *Courtesy of Allan & Laurie Carter.*

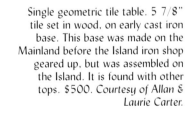

Undersea Garden table. Four tiles make the scene. This is the one of a very few examples currently known, and matching shards have also been found on Pebbly Beach. It is possible that this was the prototype, or an audition piece, upon which the undersea garden plates were based. This pie shaped tile form is not common to Catalina but has been found on the signed blue example (also pictured). Similar in shape and design to many Taylor tile sets, this unique scene has also been found (without the border design) exactly duplicated on a few unusual Undersea Garden plates. Diameter of tiles 16 1/4" including grout. N.P. *Courtesy of Paul Lenaburg & Phillip Rubin.*

Decorative tile table in wrought iron base. $800. Courtesy of John Phelps.

Hand painted Mexican Oxcart tile table. Very hard to find tile. Six tiles make the scene. Done on white glazed field tiles. No artist signature. Pasadena made vintage base with iron stretchers. This table comes in a Desert Cactus motif as well. 18" high. 12" x 18" tile set only. $2,000. Courtesy of Carole Coates.

Poinsettia tile table in iron base. Found with both orange or black center tiles. $1,500+. Courtesy of Catalina Island Museum.

Detail of Oxcart tile table.

Backgammon table in original Island iron base. NP. *Courtesy of Catalina Island Museum.*

Small tile table. Orange, yellow, and black motif with decorated center tile. Original Island Deco iron base, shown in early brochure. 18" tall. $650. *Courtesy of Carole Coates.*

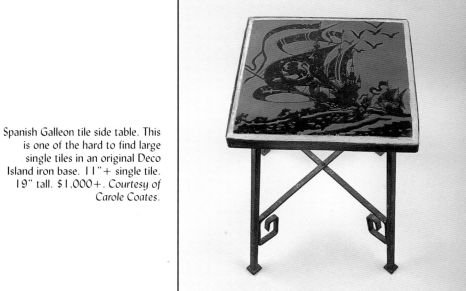

Spanish Galleon tile side table. This is one of the hard to find large single tiles in an original Deco Island iron base. 11"+ single tile. 19" tall. $1,000+. *Courtesy of Carole Coates.*

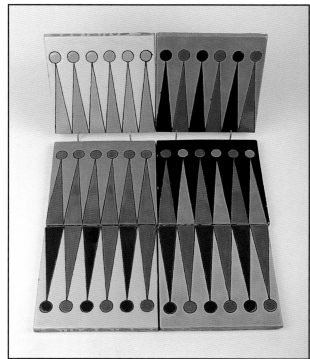

Backgammon tiles shown in different glaze colors. Six individual 8" tiles. $250 - $400 each. *Courtesy of Carole Coates.*

Marlin four tile set. On early cast iron base (not shown). 12" x 12". $3,000. *Courtesy of Jerry Kunz.*

Detail showing Marlin table's iron base.

Marlin tile table. Four 5 5/8" tiles with borders. Unusual green coloration. In iron base. $3,000+. *Courtesy of John Phelps.*

Checkerboard table in original iron base. $2,800+. *Courtesy of Carole Coates.*

Dragon tile in original Island iron smoke stand. 9" tile. Holder is 28" high to handle. NP. *Courtesy of Carole Coates.*

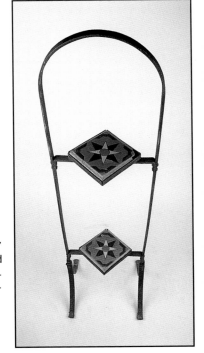

Smoke stand with bowl for ashtray. Original Island iron, but other companies made look-alikes. 22" tall. *Courtesy of Carole Coates.*

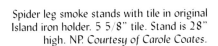

Spider leg smoke stands with tile in original Island iron holder. 5 5/8" tile. Stand is 28" high. NP. *Courtesy of Carole Coates.*

Plant holder with two 4" Star tiles. Original Island iron holder. 38" high. *Courtesy of Carole Coates.*

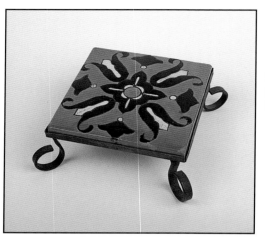

Trivet. Single iron tile holder. Other tile makers used these as well. 5" tile. $350. *Courtesy of Carole Coates.*

Unusual table lamp. Field tiles on iron base. The Island ink stamp on its base is the same as is found on a tea tile. $650. *Courtesy of Allan and Laurie Carter.*

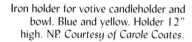

Iron holder for votive candleholder and bowl. Blue and yellow. Holder 12" high. NP. *Courtesy of Carole Coates.*

Star tile table. Nine tiles in green painted Monterey "style" wooden base. *Courtesy of Catalina Island Museum. NP.*

Monterey desk (signed) with Catalina tile and leather inset. Original painting on front drawer. $2,500. Courtesy of Bill Noonan.

Monterey Painted Prohibition Bar. When closed, it looked like a gentlemen's dresser. Topped with Catalina field tiles in orange with black borders.

A closer look at the Monterey desk.

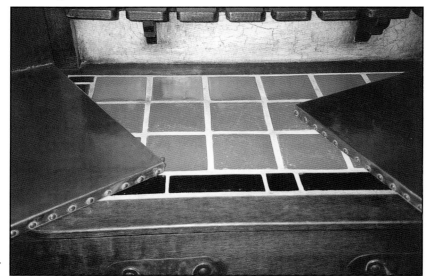

Close up view of Monterey bar top.

In 1932, the building boom in Southern California went bust and with it came the reported death of tile (Malibu 1988; Prouty, 46), coincidentally in the same year as Mr. Wrigley's passing. He died in his Phoenix, Arizona, home at the age of 71. Special tiles were commissioned for his impressive Island memorial, now the home to a world class botanical garden as well. A large inventory of tiles would sit waiting for a customer or a job, but the pottery works continued to keep the employees busy.

Wrigley Memorial, found at the end of the pathway. Home to a world class Botanical Garden with a stunning array of cactus and indigenous Catalina plants.

Catalina "Style"

Shades of Old California

In 1933, D.M. bought and created the El Encanto marketplace, which featured Spanish dancers and entertainers and created an atmosphere modeled on Los Angeles' Olvera Street. It was a big success. He brought over Mr. Jose Riojas from Olvera Street to act as its host. Mr. Riojas' daughter Millie Poindexter remembers hand painting tiles and novelties after school for sale in the shops there. The restaurant in El Encanto also had a branch in Olvera Street that was renowned for having the walls lined with Catalina hand painted vaquero plates.

"Toneful Pottery." Catalina pots accompanied musicians at the Bird Park. *Courtesy of Catalina Island Museum.*

El Encanto. Restaurant, entertainment, and shops in the "Alta California" style. *Courtesy of Catalina Island Museum.*

By 1934, Phillip Wrigley had caught the "Alta California" spirit. Otis Shepard, art director for Wrigley's Chewing Gum, and his artist wife Dorothy were brought to Avalon to help out. The main street of Avalon was renamed "Avenida de la Crescenta" and underwent a major face-lift. Maybe they were also looking for something to do with all that leftover tile. Malcolm Renton took over where his father had left off and continued the Spanish make-over, including the creation of the Airport in the Sky. But all the work was interrupted in the 1940s when the War began. In 1935 at the Panama Pacific exhibit in San Diego, Catalina Island pottery was featured, but tile was not.

The famous "Serpent" Wall, designed by Otis Shepard, still snakes its way along Avalon's Crescent Avenue. Non-vintage trash can.

Portrait of Phillip (P.K.) Wrigley. *Courtesy of Catalina Island Museum.*

The recently restored Sombrero Fountain was one of the many decorative touches put in during the "Old California" makeover begun in 1934. The old "Pottery Shop" was just across the street on the ocean side, on Casino Way. Design credited to Otis Shepard. Contemporary reproduction tiles.

Old photo showing the "Pottery Shop" with newly installed Fountain across the street. Notice all the palm trees. The building was heavily damaged by storms over the years and did not survive past the 1950s.

Another view of the Chimes Tower. Note: the teeny pot on top is actually a 17" oil jar.

Catalina Pottery Bell similar to the one found in the tower of the "Pottery Shop." Unglazed red clay. Height: 17" (not including metal). NP.

One of the more photographed spots in Avalon. Two views. Plaza Fountain is dedicated to explorer Juan Cabrillo, whose death is ironically said to have been hastened when he took a fall while fleeing the Island. He died from an infection shortly thereafter on another Channel Island. Historic tiles and shards adorn the inside and top of the fountain. Contemporary reproduction tiles on the exterior.

Bird Mural tiles utilized in large planter box. Lined with concrete.
Courtesy of Sandra Puttnam.
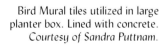

The Final Years
The Deco Line and Transitional Wares

Virgil Haldeman is credited with developing the lighter glazes used on the Starlight, Rope, and later Deco lines which were produced in 1936 even though he supposedly stopped working for Catalina in 1933. At that time Haldeman began Caliente Pottery, which made vases, tableware, and figurines and which closed up shop in 1953. He used many forms and glazes inspired by his work on the Island and made pottery souvenirs, using close cousins of the Catalina glaze colors. Caliente items such as bunnies, elephants, and sailboats have appeared with stickers from Catalina shops, so it seems likely that he had a continuing association with the pottery works.

D.M. Renton lost his wife in 1935, and by 1936 decided to retire. His son Malcolm took over his duties and became assistant to Phillip Wrigley, who was then President of the Santa Catalina Island Company. Phillip Wrigley (b.12/05/1894, d. 4/12/77),

whose contributions and influence on Catalina were to span nearly 60 years, was ably assisted by Malcolm Renton (b.1/16/08, d.8/1/97) who continued to call Avalon home for the rest of his life. There was no one with the zeal for the pottery to take D.M.'s place, plus it was not a huge money-maker, and so the search was begun for a company to utilize the plant and keep the local workers employed. Competitor and takeover king Gladding McBean saw the advantage in buying the name yet declined to use the plant. They already had one. After almost a year of negotiations the deal was sealed. Gladding McBean used some molds and kept the Catalina name in use for a few years until their own similar line took hold. The pottery closed for good in April 1937. The last months had consisted of only a few employees glazing the remaining stock on hand. (Hall letters, 1937).

Handled Deco vase in later light blue. *Courtesy of Jerry Kunz.*

Shell serving dishes and handled bud vases. 9" long & vases, transitional 700 and 800 series. Pieces currently believed to have been made on the Island prior to Gladding, McBean's purchase. Pink, turquoise, and yellow. 5" high. $75 - $125. *Courtesy of Jerry Kunz.*

Starlight candleholders and vase combination. Light blue. 4" high. $175 pair. *Courtesy of Jerry Kunz.*

Deco vase selection. Turquoise and yellow. Ranging from 7" to 5". $100 - $275. *Courtesy of Jerry Kunz.*

Various "Deco" styled vases. White and ivory glazes. Ranging in height from 8 1/4" to 5" high. $100 - $400. *Courtesy of Allan & Laurie Carter.*

Top: Deco vases. Red and light blue. 6" and 5". $165 and $195. *Courtesy of Carole Coates.*

Bottom: Variety of "Deco" vases. Mandarin yellow. Ranging from 7 5/8" to 5 5/8". $200 to $500. *Courtesy of John Phelps.*

Top: Starlight design bowl. These are the only Island pieces that are two toned. Not often found. White and pink. Marked "Catalina Island 709". These are transitional pieces. 10" across. NP. *Courtesy of Jerry Kunz.*

Bottom: Vase and candleholder. Transitional period two toned colors. Looks like Gladding, McBean but signed "Catalina Island", and *not* "Pottery". 10 1/4" & 4 1/2". NP. *Courtesy of Sandy Puttnam.*

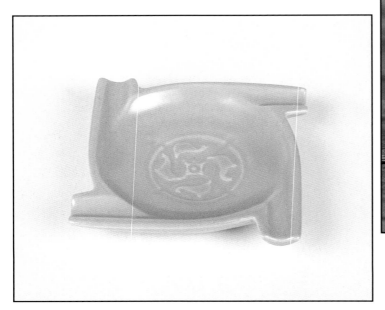

Deco line ashtray. Light blue. 4". $60. *Courtesy of Jerry Kunz.*

Interesting comparison. Catalina Pelican, white. A light green Pelican figurine believed to be Caliente, and two known Caliente swans in the same glaze. NP. *Courtesy of Carole Coates.*

Is it "Island" or is it "Pottery"? Island serving bowl and Gladding McBean coaster with raised sawtooth border design. Both an identical match in Turquoise. Transitional period. "Catalina Island 721" on bowl and "GMB" ink stamp on coaster. 14" & 4". $150 and $20. *Courtesy of Jerry Kunz.*

Caliente Bunnies. Sold on Catalina Island. Almost identical to Catalina glazes. 5 1/2" tall. $100+.

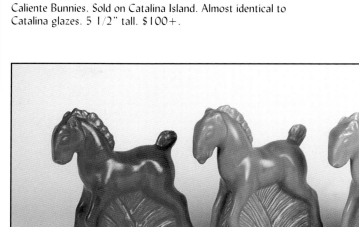

Base of white Bunny showing Caliente numbering. Others not marked.

Deco Horse figurines. Possibly Caliente. Wonderful detail. Sold on the Island, often in pairs. Red, green, and turquoise. 6" tall. 4 1/2" base. NP.

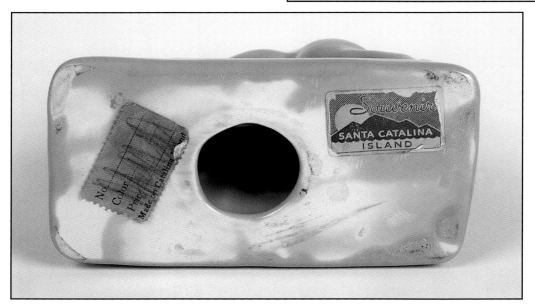

Bottom of Horse with sticker and price tag.

Caliente Sailboat. Turquoise. No numbers or signature. Exact form as Haldeman's Caliente Sailboat flower frog. 6" tall. $65. *Courtesy of Allan & Laurie Carter.*

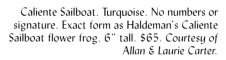

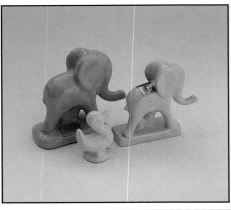

Caliente Elephant in pink glaze, transitional smaller Elephant and Caliente Duck in Caliente soft yellow glaze. Small Elephant sold on the Island.

Detail of figurine bottoms with stickers.

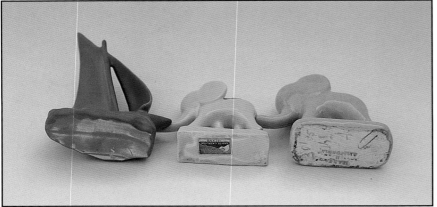

Later Pottery Souvenirs *not made* by Catalina, but by other California pottery companies, including Cemar.

Obscurity and Rediscovery

Civilians were evacuated from the Island in 1941 after Japanese subs were supposedly sighted off the California coast. With the start of World War II, women and children were sent "overtown," the luxury steamers were painted battleship gray, and a patriotic Phillip Wrigley rented out hotels as barracks facilities to the armed services. The Island was used as both an outpost and training facility. Many of the people with knowledge of the pottery and tile works left during this time, some never to return.

In December of 1941, employees of the Island Company were sent to the old pottery storage rooms to destroy the molds that had not been taken by Gladding McBean. The plaster of paris molds broke very easily when they were thrown into the dump. (Lopez Sr. Interview 2000)

After the factory closed, some residents remember being allowed to fill up a pick up truck with tiles for $5. Many Islanders used these leftovers to tile their pathways, garden borders, steps, and patios.

Islander John Phelps, a major Monterey Brown collector and a contributor to this book, remembers with much chagrin that sometime in the 1950s he edged a pallet of vintage tile murals and decorative sets into the sea. They were getting in everyone's way at the wood saw near the old furniture factory.

When California pottery experts Jack Chipman and Judy Stangler went to Avalon in the late 1970s to research Catalina pottery, the Chamber of Commerce and the Library told them that "there wasn't any pottery factory here." When asked where all the colorful pots and tiles had come from helpful residents guessed "Los Angeles?" and referred them to Bud Upton as someone who might know "something about something." (Chipman Interview 2000) With that and articles written by Patricia Moore of the Catalina Island Museum, more facts began to emerge.

The factory was NOT all bulldozed into the sea as has been commonly thought. Pottery plant buildings and parts of buildings still remain tucked among the Helicopter Pad and electrical facility at Pebbly Beach, many reincarnated for new and different uses. Housing that was built for workers at the plant so they could be near enough to check on the kilns at all hours still stand in two neat rows.

Tiled garden steps. *Courtesy of Sandra Puttnam.*

One of the remnants of the pottery plant and tile factory. Possibly the showroom.

The Workers Stories

Some say that the term "California Antique" is an oxymoron since the state is so relatively young, but luckily for us our history is recent enough to enable us to find some living employees and relatives of workers who were associated with the pottery. The overriding feeling one gets when hearing their stories is that they were like a family. Many *were* family members. During these rough economic times, the Wrigley's and Renton's drummed up work to keep "their people" employed.

Group photograph including Claire Hall (fourth from the right, top row), and Joe Saucedo (fifth from the left, top row). Research continues and the author would greatly appreciate being contacted by anyone with information about people in this photo for future editions.

POTTERY PLANT EMPLOYEES – 1936 & 1937

Letters were sent by Malcolm J. Renton to Mr. Pendroy at Gladding, McBean and Company only for those employees who were seeking work in the ceramic business. This is a partial list of those employed by the plant during the last year of it's operation. Some decided to stay on the Island, some declined letters and pursued other interests on the mainland. Of the employees recommended many had long careers with Gladding McBean and Franciscan in Glendale until the 1950s.

Helen Southwick	Casting dept., small items and novelties 1931-37
Nick Garcia*	Spray Man 1937
Oliver T. Quinn	Jiggerman, 1932-1937
Lucy Watkins	Flowers and Novelties designer, 1932-37
Adella Machado*	Finisher in Casting Dept., 1937
W.E. Robinson	Jiggerman, 1935-37
Claire E. Hall*	Pottery Sprayer, 1934-37
C.B. Powell	Glaze dipper, 1934-37
Vernon Wharton	Casting and cup handler, 1937
Sam Young	Jiggerman, 1935-37
Harold M. Hall*	Glaze Sprayer, 1936-37
Paul Valencia	Kiln Setter, Brick & Tile Machine, 1930-37
Velma Mayberry	Jigger finisher, 1934-37
Orville Davidson	Casting Department, 1934-37
Jose Saucedo*	Spray man, 1937
Concha Liceaga	Novelties, 1937
Don Ruth	Mold Maker, 1937
Dan Rios	Kiln setter, 1928-37
M.L. Cueva*	Kiln setter, 1936-37
George Seale	Kiln setter, 1928-37
Harry S. Allan	Kiln Fireman
Harry Parson	Kiln Fireman
Cy Scarratt	Kiln Fireman
Karl Ozenghar*	Bisque Warehouse
Stella Van Treese	Bisque Warehouse
Peggy Machada*	Bisque Warehouse
Rosabelle Harter	Bisque Warehouse
Byron Chase*	Lab
Joe Machado*	Kiln setter
J. Purcell	Spraying Glaze
Vincent Marincovich	Finishing Finished Ware
John Peterson	Finishing Finished Ware
L.H. Burkitt	Office

The Hall Family

The Hall family histories include a rich abundance of stories relating to Catalina's pottery and tile plant and bring rare first hand accounts and a realistic look at the times. An effort was made to hire people of high caliber, in terms of morals and work ethic, and so family members and close friends that were personally recommended by trusted employees had the best chance to secure a job. At least four members of the Hall family worked at or for the pottery.

Maude Chase's brother Claire (born Clarence) Hall came to Catalina in the early 1930s when he was in his late 40s. It was a tough time financially for many and the Halls had experienced quite a comedown. The well-to-do family had settled in Santa Ana; but, the Depression caused their family owned bank to close, Claire lost his bakery business, and although they owned property, most family members felt lucky to have jobs at all.

Harold Hall, wife Dorothy, and daughter "Babe" (Virginia). Taken near the Bird Park, 1939. *Courtesy of Don Hall.*

"Uncle" Byron Chase and his niece, Johnette, at the Bird Park. *Courtesy of Johnette Eilert.*

Claire was a pottery sprayer for Catalina from 1934-1937 and had earlier worked in the quarry. His 27 year old son Harold, Maude Chase's nephew, worked for the power plant but joined his dad at the pottery in 1936 as a glaze sprayer. Harold's young wife and new baby daughter Virginia lived on the Island with him. After the pottery closed in 1937, Claire went to work for Gladding McBean in Glendale until the 1950s when he retired. He died in 1974 in Lancaster, California, where his son Don Hall worked for NASA on some of the top rocket and shuttle projects of our time. Claire's son Harold stayed on at the Island's power plant until World War II when women and children were evacuated. Harold then worked for Douglas Aircraft (as did Maude and Byron) until he died in 1963 at the age of 52. Maude is of course the "Chase" that is known for her beautifully hand painted Catalina plates. (see "Chase" profile earlier) In family letters Claire worried as the pottery was coming to a close in early 1937 whether he would receive a job with Gladding McBean or not. Family letters discuss the pottery colors that were their favorites and how they loved to buy the factory "seconds." They mentioned disappointment when the wonderful "new" color, Monterey Brown, was discontinued. They also gave each other pottery sets as

gifts and coveted certain items they hoped to someday own. Maude Chase made special plate and cup "sets" for each of her grandchildren that she had hand-painted with then-popular cartoon characters. They are still cherished to this day as family heirlooms. Claire experimented with many two-toned glaze combinations that were quite unusual, using black and yellow, or blue and yellow.

Claire Hall's experimental two toned pottery. Footed, fluted bowl, Starlight candleholder vase, and salt and pepper shakers. Black and yellow glaze. NP.

Experimental two toned pottery. Two bowls, rope cup and saucer, and Fish humidor with lid. NP.

Claire Hall, and his ever present hat, at work spraying pottery. *Courtesy of Catalina Island Museum.*

The Ozenghar Family

Ken Ozenghar was a baby and his sister was a young schoolgirl at the time their father Karl was in charge of the bisque warehouse from 1933 to 1937. Ken's strong memory is that the employees were a close knit group. During cold nights, they would sometimes walk out to the plant and sit in the still warm kilns while the people on the late shift worked inside the other buildings. Ken's mother Thelma also did some painting and design work, while the kids sold seashells to the many movie people and stars that went there in droves. Everyone did their part to contribute.

Vince Davis and Al Oldham

Al Oldham was only 12 years old in 1929 when he worked with his Uncle Vince Davis on the Island. At the time, Mr. Davis was the kiln master for the pottery plant. They lived in the worker housing built at Pebbly Beach. Mr. Oldham, now 83 years old, went to a boarding school in Northern California after his mother died. Al's Dad, Hardin Duke "Tex" Oldham, had been a Texas Ranger and he worked at the Island Villas as a "roustabout," kind of a combination peacekeeper and handyman. Vince Davis and "Tex" Oldham were brothers-in-law (Mr. Davis had married Tex's sister) and they both got jobs on the Island after seeing an advertisement in a Wilmington, California, paper.

Young Al didn't like school. For many years, when spring came, his dad brought him to Catalina and kept him busy at the pottery with his uncle. Al remembers stacking dishes hot out of the kiln at Pebbly Beach almost every day. He was impressed that D.M. Renton, the "big boss," asked him "So, how do you like the job?" even though Al was just a kid. Al remembers helping to plant some of the palm trees in 1932 for the Avenida de la Crescenta project. He enjoyed very much when he and his dad were able to watch the Cubs in Spring Training and remembers seeing Mr. Wrigley riding through town on his horse. "We saw him all the time. It was no big deal," he says. "Mr. Wrigley loved the Bird Farm. He just hung out there." (Oldham interview 2000)

Al went back to Avalon on and off until his father left in the mid-thirties when D.M. did (it is also believed that Mr. Davis passed away sometime prior to 1936), but he remembers one special trip in 1938. This time he was stacking and washing dishes at the Casino ballroom kitchen. Al was one of Catalina's earliest "collectors." His Uncle Vince had always brought home test pieces of new items that were being tried out, as well as "after hours" work, and Al inherited some of this pottery. Also, as a truck driver in four western states, he'd stop at every roadside "junk house" to look for it. No one else knew about it or wanted the old "stuff," but Al's fond memories of the Island inspired him to collect many examples. One of Vince Davis' pieces of Catalina helped to solve the mystery of the rare Casino humidors. One of the most elusive

of Catalina pottery pieces, none was signed "Catalina." Instead, they had different first names and last initials. Examining the existing Casinos turned up names such as Joe M. and Karl and Thelma. These are all names that coincide with known pottery company employees. Upon inquiring if they were perhaps special gifts to employees, Al recalled that the piece was made by one of the designers (exactly who is unknown, perhaps mold maker Don Ruth) who gave them as birthday presents.

The Machado Family

Joe Machado worked for the pottery for many years. His nephew Frank, an Islander who recently retired to the mainland, remembers him fondly. Joe's daughters Peggy and Adella worked at the pottery. Their cousin Manganito Cuevas worked in the kilns. Yet again we find one extended family that includes 4 or 5 employees. Frank's dad came to Catalina in 1924, the year Frank was born, and worked for Graham Brothers in the quarry. The brothers would sometimes go and get clay for the two big kilns. He remembers seeing Mr. Wrigley, who used to delight the children by throwing nickels and pennies to them. He remembers going out to where the pottery kept the "seconds" next to the edge of the water. It was okay to take them home, and since the factory was very picky most just had a minor scratch or bubble. Sometimes they'd take a plate or two and skip them out over the ocean. Today Frank's son collects Catalina Island Pottery.

Joe Saucedo

Joe Saucedo and Al Oldham are among the few known living employees of the pottery plant. Gloria Lopez and Bernice Limbeck Gallant are also still around and kicking and have been interviewed in the past regarding their memories of being brought in for tile glaze work done specifically for the Wrigley Memorial. Joe is currently 90 years old and living in Southern California. He goes to Avalon yearly to visit family members that live on the Island.

Conclusion
Endangered Tiles Challenges and Solutions

The Wrigley influence continues as a major factor in Catalina's future. The Island we see today has been preserved much as it was in the thirties, due in large part to their positive examples and an amazingly visionary environmentalism. William Wrigley Jr., Phillip Wrigley, and the Catalina Island Company are owed a large debt of gratitude that there is so much original "charm" left to Avalon. Refreshingly, the merchants have kept the taffy store and shut out the fast food vendors and chain stores that make many towns into "Anywhere USA."

Fountain / Planter in tour bus terminal with three Bird Murals. Successfully relocated from the Bird Park.

But for some there is concern that no safeguards are in place to conserve or relocate existing historic tile installations. Despite much hue and cry on the mainland and many impassioned articles, the challenge still remains: how to keep the heritage of Catalina Island tile a treasured legacy for all to enjoy on the Island without intruding on the needs of Avalon as a living, working city. To accomplish this, the distinction should be made between conservation and preservation. Conservation is a more moderate and practical approach. Some important installations have been "conserved" and moved with great success, but it is greatly hoped that either the Avalon City Council or the Island Museum will take the lead in instituting a workable policy for historic tile conservation before it is too late. These tiles represent the cultural and social fabric of their times, but this is an Island issue that cannot be solved by outsiders. Avalon, the city, cannot be subject to delays, expenses, or interference in its normal functioning. But those of us "overtown" can indeed help by covering any expenses involved in removing and/or reinstalling historic tiles caught in the way of progress. Many collectors and tile enthusiasts would be happy to sponsor or "adopt" tile works that are in jeopardy on the Island. Tile removal specialists must be called in to rescue historic tiles since a particular expertise is required to remove them or they will be destroyed in the process, as past vandalism has shown. Tiles can either be reinstalled, if practical, or donated to the Island Museum for display. The main goal here should be protection, not plunder, but in certain instances, auctioning vintage tiles to the highest bidder, with the proceeds going to charitably benefit Avalon's schools, might be a viable alternative.

This is not a false alarm. In the ten short years since Lee Rosenthal's *Catalina Tile* book was published, many of the irreplaceable Island tile installations she photographed have become extinct. The famous El Encanto tower was removed and demolished. The Country Club had been in jeopardy but luckily was saved and even earthquake retrofitted. Today it is a fabulous restaurant for dinner or special events, as well as a golf center. The fantastic Crane Mural water fountain was preserved, but the quirky men's bathroom wall and the patio floor didn't make it. Perhaps parts of them were saved or fell into private hands. Mr. Wrigley's beloved Bird Park is in a sad state, with gorgeous bird murals, original hand painted interior borders, tile counters, and rare single tiles in immediate danger of being incorporated into a much needed housing project. It is not known what the plans are for Las Casitas, the historic bungalow housing of the Chicago Cubs, except that a municipal office building is due to be constructed on that site. Las Casitas contains some one-of-a-kind tiles embedded in walls, inside and out. Hopefully the option of moving and restoring these tiles or buildings will be considered.

Country Club floor.

Decorative tile planter box.

Decorative tile wall with two Bird Murals at Bird Park.

Las Casitas sign.

The Bird Park.

Decorative tile wall with Toucan Mural at Bird Park.

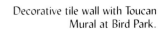

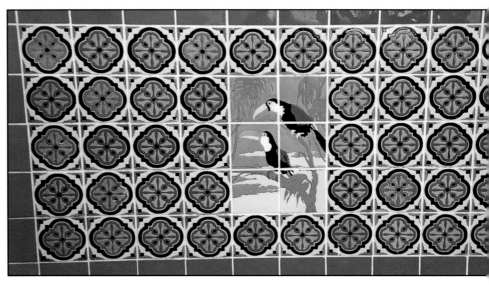

The Avalon community understands the vital importance its heritage adds to the Island's allure and also the marketing spin that comes with having an authentic "old town" with credentials to rival Pasadena. Avalon is "retro" without trying and many visitors today go to Avalon to see the tiles and the architecture. A few islanders still take the pottery and tile for granted and don't see what all the fuss is about. They have been seeing it, even eating on it, for years. "That old stuff?" is one reaction, and they certainly are not aware of the prices some of these rarities command. It is also hard for some to take seriously buildings and tile installations that were created in a "recent" history that many still recall. Others proudly display their cherished family collection that has been handed down from generation to generation. The Catalina Island Museum has done a wonderful job in increasing "tile" awareness and conducts a yearly in-depth exhibit and seminar every September that is a must-see. They currently do not have the space to keep all of their impressive collection on display (including some classic memorabilia) on a year-round basis. As awareness has increased, certain harmful practices have stopped. You definitely won't see "sandblast" cleaning of tiles or street sweeper trucks taking the corners off vintage tile buildings as had happened in the past.

There are many new tile installations that have been added to the town, some in "replacement" of old, authentic tiles. But historic tiles cannot truly be "replaced." Once gone, they are gone forever. A reproduction of a historic tile, no matter how well done, is still a copy. This is not to take away from the original art tile that has been created for the Island in recent years, much of it excellent and in keeping with the tile tradition of the town.

RTK Studios' 140 foot long mural in the wall on the Island's Casino Way, done by Richard Keit and Mary Richards of Ojai, California, has world class artistic merit of its own. It is a brilliant reinterpretation of vintage postcards with Island scenes, as well as original ocean life pictorials. No doubt RTK's work will be collected and sought after in years to come. A painted tile mural in an archway over the entrance to the Island Company's Discover Tours building, done by artist Will Richards, beautifully reinterprets an original Otis Shepard design of the town. Marlo Bartels has done some stunning work around town, as has Miller Art Tile. The Green Pleasure Pier has new tile installations that make even the bathrooms a "must see." Larry Harris' recent book on Island tile focuses on new and historic installations and includes helpful maps for "tile tours."

Contemporary tile mural. Hamilton Cove, based on vintage postcard. Installed on Casino Way, Avalon. This is one of a series done by RTK Studios, Ojai, California.

Contemporary tile mural. Glass bottom boat view. Big Mouth Bass in porthole. Installed on Casino Way, Avalon. Another series by RTK Studios.

Catalina's pottery and historic tile has found its way into museum collections and displays in Santa Barbara, Santa Monica, and Oakland alongside other art movements of the era. It is hoped that this book will prompt further creative thinking of new ways we can maintain Avalon's ceramic heritage for future generations to see and appreciate not *only* in museums. D.M. Renton observed in his autobiography ". . . we created a demand for the pottery that has advertised Catalina far more than it was given credit for." Like many art forms that aren't fully appreciated until given the test of time, the long overdue credit is being given today in full recognition of Catalina Island's ceramic heritage.

People who wold like to support conservation of Historic Catalina tile may send donations to The Catalina Island Museum Society, P.O. Box 366, Avalon, CA 90704. Ask for your contribution to be earmarked for future tile conservation efforts. You can also help the Museum by becoming a member and should visit them in the Casino on the Island as well as on their web site at http://www.catalina.com/museum.html for further information.

There are Tile Awareness and Education organizations that exist today but the author currently knows of no group that is specifically devoted to California tile conservation. The author is willing to connect persons interested in starting such a group, a California Art Tile Society, that would be created for the purpose of identifying, conserving, and raising funds *only* for the repair or relocation of endangered historic tile installations. Please contact her at P.O. Box 75, Kenwood, CA 95452 or at potteryhound@aol.com.

The sun sets on a "Catalina" soda display case filled with pottery, not soda.

Avalon Bay.

Bibliography

Baizerman, Suzanne, Lynn Downey, and John Toki. *Fired By Ideals. Arequipa Pottery and the Arts and Crafts Movement.* November 2000 exhibition held at the Oakland Museum of California. Rohnert Park, CA: Pomegranate Communications, Inc., 2000.

Chipman, Jack. *Collector's Encyclopedia of California Pottery, Second Edition.* Paducah, KY: Collector Books, 1999.

Fridley, Al. *Catalina Pottery: The Early Years, 1927-1937.* Los Angeles: A.W. Fridley. 1977.

Harris, Larry. *The Jewels of Avalon, Decorative Tiles of Catalina Island.* 1999.

Held, Wilbur. Collectible Caliente Pottery - Made by the Haldeman Potteries. Privately printed. 1987 and 1997.

Hoefs, Steven and Aisha. *Catalina Island Pottery Collectors Guide.* 1993.

Karlson, Norman. *American Art Tile, 1876-1941.* New York, New York: Rizzoli International Publications, Inc., 1998.

Monterey Furnishings of California's Spanish Revival. In cooperation with the California Heritage Museum. Atgen, PA.: Schiffer Publishing Ltd., 2000.

Renton, D.M. Autobiography. 1939. From *Santa Catalina Island: It's Magic, People and History* by Ernest Windle. (1931)

Rindge, Ronald L. *Ceramic Art of the Malibu Potteries 1926-1932.* Malibu, California: The Malibu Lagoon Museum, 1988,

_____. *More about Malibu Potteries 1926-1932.* Malibu, California: The Malibu Lagoon Museum, 1997.

Rosenthal, Lee. *Catalina Tiles of the Magic Isle.* Sausalito, California: Windgate Press, 1992.

Sexton, R.W. *Spanish Influence on American Architecture and Decoration.* New York, NY: Brentano's, 1927.

White, William S. with Tice, Steven K. *Santa Catalina Island: It's Magic, People and History.* 2nd Edition. Glendora, California: White Limited Editions, 2000.

Windle, Ernest. *Windle's History of Catalina Island.* Avalon, California: The Catalina Islander publ., 1931.

Zimmerman, William, Jr. *William Wrigley, Jr.: The Man and His Business 1861-1932.* Chicago: Private Printing. 1935.

Oral Histories/Interviews

All Interviews conducted by the author either in person or by telephone unless otherwise stated.

Chipman, Jack. Interviews with the author. 1996-2000.

Gilert, Johnette. Interview with the author. December 2000.

Hall, Don. Interviews and family correspondence with the author. September-October 2000.

Kaiser, Brian. Interview with the author. November 2000.

Kaylor, Joan. Interview with the author. December 2000.

Lopez, Pastor, Sr. Interview with the author. Avalon, California, July, September, and December 2000.

Machado, Frank. Interview with the author. November 2000.

Oldham, Al. Interview and correspondence with the author. October - December 2000.

Ozenghar, Ken. Interview with the author. October 2000.

Renton, Dave. Correspondence with the author. 2000.

Upton, Roger, Jr. Interview with the author. September 2000.

Whittaker, Dick. Interviews. September & December 2000.

Windle, Johnny and Jean. Interview with the author. July 1998.

Articles, Periodicals and Other

Material

Advertisement. "C.R. Kayser & Company 4405 Fruitland Ave., Los Angeles, Sole Distributors of Catalina Tables." February 1932.

Bevil, Alexander D. Bevil. "The History of the California China Products Company of National City, California 1911-1917." *The Journal of San Diego History*, Vol. 45, Number 4, Fall 1999.

Catalina Islander. "Catalina Tile, Brick and Novelty Factory Now In Operation—kilns being built." July 1927.

_____. "Catalina Branch Bank Thoroughly Up to Date." September 1930.

_____. "Catalina Pottery is now displayed in Los Angeles." September 1931.

_____. "Catalina Tables Attract Much Attention." February 1932.

Fortune. "William Wrigley Jr., American." April 1932. pp. 96-99.

Los Angeles Times. "Bogged Auto Starts New Industry." October 9, 1932.

Overholt, Alma. "Catalina Pottery Gaining Buyers Who Seek 'Finds'." *Catalina Islander*, November 1931.

Overholt, Alma. "Catalina Pottery Big Island Asset." *Catalina Islander*, December 1931.

Overholt, Alma. "Catalina Pottery Wins First Place." *Catalina Islander*, March 1932.

Overholt, Alma. "Color to Order: Pottery Reflects our Joyous Moods." *Catalina Islander*, December 1932.

Towne, Robert. "Chinatown-A Screenwriter's Eulogy for Los Angeles." *Architectural Digest*, April 2000.

Southwestern Purchasing Agent. Smith, Al J. "'In All the World No Trip Like This'. Catalina Lures Purchasing Agents and Cost Accountants." April 1932.

William Wrigley Jr. and David M. Renton Correspondence, Letters from 1919 to 1932. From the Malcolm J. Renton Collection.

Index